Microwave Cooking Chart for Vegetables

Cooking vegetables in the microwave is the best way to preserve nutrients and flavor, and often the quickest way to cook them. Cook all the vegetables at HIGH power in a baking dish covered with wax paper. If you use plastic wrap to cover the dish, be sure to turn back one corner to allow steam to escape.

Food	Microwave Cooking Time	Special Instructions
Asparagus, 1 pound	6 to 7 minutes	Add ¼ cup water
Beans, green, 1 pound	14 to 15 minutes	Add ½ cup water
Broccoli spears, 1 pound	7 to 8 minutes	Arrange in a circle, spoke-fashion, with flowerets in center; add ½ cup water
Carrot slices, 1 pound	9 to 10 minutes; stand 2 minutes	Add ¼ cup water
Cauliflower flowerets, 1 pound	7 to 8 minutes; stand 2 minutes	Add ¼ cup water
Corn on the cob, 2 (large) ears 3 ears 4 ears	5 to 9 minutes 7 to 12 minutes 8 to 15 minutes	Arrange end-to-end in a circle; add ¼ cup water
Onions, peeled and quartered, 1 pound	6 to 8 minutes	Add 2 tablespoons water
Peas, green, shelled, 1 pound (about 1½ cups)	6 to 7 minutes	Add 2 tablespoons water
Potatoes, baking/sweet, medium 1 potato 2 potatoes 4 potatoes	4 to 6 minutes 7 to 8 minutes 12 to 14 minutes	Pierce skins and arrange end-to-end in a circle; let stand 5 minutes after cooking
New potatoes, 1 pound	8 to 10 minutes	Pierce if unpeeled; add ¼ cup water
Spinach, 10-ounce package fresh leaves ·	2 to 3 minutes	Wash leaves before cooking
Squash, Yellow/Zucchini, 1 pound, sliced (4 medium)	7 to 8 minutes	Add ¼ cup water
Squash, Acorn, 2 pounds, (2 medium)	9 to 10 minutes	Pierce skins
Turnips, 1¼ pounds, peeled and cubed (4 medium)	10 to 12 minutes	Add ¼ cup water

**Southwestern Corn and
Red Pepper Soup**
recipe, page 158

Pineapple-Mint Ice
recipe, page 38

Gingered Grapefruit Sorbet
recipe, page 36

Minted Watermelon Granita
recipe, page 37

Tortellini with Swiss Chard
recipe, page 82

3

**Bourbon Pork Tenderloin
with Peach Chutney**
recipe, page 105

Weight Watchers®

Miracle Foods

More Fruits, More Veggies

Oxmoor House®

Library of Congress Control Number: 2001-132436
ISBN: 0-8487-2432-1
Printed in the United States of America
First Printing 2001

Be sure to check with your health-care provider before making any changes in your diet.

Weight Watchers® is a registered trademark of Weight Watchers International, Inc., and is used under license by Healthy Living, Inc.

Editor-in-Chief: Nancy Fitzpatrick Wyatt
Senior Foods Editor: Katherine M. Eakin
Senior Editor, Copy and Homes: Olivia Kindig Wells
Art Director: James Boone

Weight Watchers Miracle Foods: More Fruits, More Veggies

Editor: Suzanne Henson, M.S., R.D.
Associate Art Director: Cynthia R. Cooper
Designer: Clare T. Minges
Copy Editors: Heather Averett, Jacqueline Giovanelli
Editorial Assistant: Suzanne Powell
Director, Test Kitchens: Elizabeth Tyler Luckett
Assistant Director, Test Kitchens: Julie Christopher
Recipe Editor: Gayle Hays Sadler
Test Kitchens Staff: Donna Baldone; Jennifer Cofield;
   Gretchen P. Feldtman, R.D.; David Gallent; Ana Kelly; Rebecca Mohr Boggan; Jan A. Smith
Photographer: Brit Huckabay
Photo Stylists: Virginia R. Cravens, Ashley J. Wyatt
Publishing Systems Administrator: Rick Tucker
Director, Production and Distribution: Phillip Lee
Production Coordinator: Leslie Wells Johnson
Production Assistant: Faye Porter Bonner

Contributors:
Copy Editor and Indexer: Mary Ann Laurens
Photo Stylists: Melanie J. Clarke, Mary Lyn H. Jenkins
Recipe Development: Patti A. Bess; Jan Hanby; Nancy Hughes; Lorrie Hulston Corvin; Jean Kressy; Kathleen Royal Phillips
Test Kitchens: Alyssa Ouverson; Kate M. Wheeler, R.D.

Cover: Honeyed Salmon over Minted Citrus Salad, page 60
Back Cover: Pineapple-Mint Ice, page 38; Gingered Grapefruit Sorbet, page 36; Minted Watermelon Granita, page 37

We're Here for You!
We at Oxmoor House are dedicated to serving you with reliable information that expands your imagination and enriches your life. We welcome your comments and suggestions. Please write us at:

Oxmoor House, Inc.
Editor, *Weight Watchers Miracle Foods:*
   More Fruits, More Veggies
2100 Lakeshore Drive
Birmingham, AL 35209

To order additional publications, call 1-205-445-6560.

For more books to enrich your life, visit
oxmoorhouse.com

Contents

Introduction

Recipes

6 Six Simple Tips for Smart Eating

Eating healthfully isn't about sacrifice or denial. Rather, it's about great taste and enjoyment, variety, moderation, and balance. Fruits and vegetables, whether fresh, frozen, canned, or dried, are a great way to add variety to your meals year-round. By filling up on these flavorful foods, you'll boost the nutrients in your diet, reduce your fat intake, and possibly prevent weight gain.

All fruits and vegetables are loaded with nutrients and other protective properties necessary for good health. Our registered dietitians identified six sound tips to help you include more fruits and vegetables in your diet. Use these simple ideas as your guide to good (and good-for-you) eating:

1 Tame your appetite

Don't deny your appetite, satisfy it. If your hunger often rages out of control, tame it by filling up on fruits and vegetables. Fruits and veggies take longer to eat than fat- and calorie-laden snack foods and are rich in appetite-suppressing fiber, so you'll feel full on less food.

2 Color your plate

Nutritionally speaking, the more colorful the food, the more vitamins, minerals, and other nutrients it contains. Consider sweet potatoes, strawberries, and spinach. Those nutritional powerhouses are crammed with health benefits and flavor. The next time you sit down to a meal, take a look at your plate. Pick the foods with the brightest colors, and you'll be assured you're getting the nutrients you need for lifelong good health.

3 Take a tomato

From salsa to sauce, tomatoes are among the best foods you can eat. While tomatoes are high in vitamin C, they are prized for their lycopene content. This nutrient has cancer-fighting properties that may actually increase when tomatoes are cooked or canned.

4 Pick a berry

You don't have to live on whole wheat bread to get enough fiber in your diet. From the tiny blueberry to sweet strawberries, berries of all types are packed with important vitamins and minerals. They're also loaded with fiber. So spoon sliced strawberries over low-fat ice cream, or top angel food cake with a simple blueberry sauce. You'll get the fiber you need and the flavor you crave.

5 Eat more

Don't focus on cutting fat and calories from your diet. Instead, create healthy eating habits by increasing the variety of foods in your dietary repertoire. If you pile your plate with plenty of good-for-you foods, you'll enjoy an abundance of flavors while getting more nutrients.

6 Trim little, cook quick

Leave the peel on fresh fruits and vegetables, whenever possible. This ups your fiber intake and insures nutrients such as flavonoids stay intact. And overcooking destroys some vitamins, so cook fruits and vegetables just until crisp-tender. Steam or microwave fruits and veggies without water if possible.

test your food IQ

If you are what you eat, then it pays to know as much as you can about the foods you choose. Here's a quick quiz to boost your nutrition know-how.

1

Which contains beta-carotene?
a) cantaloupe
b) carrot
c) sweet potato
d) spinach

Answer: all of the above. The antioxidant beta-carotene is a plant pigment prized for its possible ability to protect against heart disease and certain types of cancer. It's easily recognized by its characteristic deep-orange or deep-yellow color, obvious in cantaloupe, sweet potato, carrot, mango, and papaya. However, that color is masked in spinach by a dark green pigment.

2

Which has the most fiber?
a) a bowl of shredded wheat cereal
b) a cup of blackberries
c) a cucumber
d) a cup of lettuce

Answer: b. All berries are rich fiber sources, and blackberries lead the way. One cup of blackberries packs 40% more fiber than a bowl of shredded whole wheat cereal.

3

Which of these foods packs the greatest antioxidant punch?
a) whole wheat bread
b) carrots
c) blueberries
d) oranges

Answer: c. The blueberry crams a lot of nutrients into its small size. Blueberries are rich in the antioxidant vitamins C and E. Due to their deep-blue color, blueberries also contain compounds called anthocyanins. These plant-based nutrients boast cardiovascular benefits. They also protect the body from free radical damage and may discourage blood clots from forming.

4

Which of these foods is a good source of vitamin C?
a) citrus fruits (lemons, grapefruits, oranges)
b) bell peppers
c) milk
d) broccoli

Answer: a, b, and d. Citrus fruits are well-known for their vitamin C content. Though less famous than lemons and oranges, bell peppers and broccoli also are good sources of this important nutrient. Vitamin C helps to maintain healthy skin, bones, and muscles. It also helps keep the immune system strong.

5

What's the best way to preserve the vitamin C in fruits and vegetables?
a) store them on the countertop
b) place them in a sunny window
c) cook in boiling water
d) keep them in the crisper drawer of the refrigerator

Answer: d. Preserve this antioxidant by storing vitamin C-containing fruits and vegetables in the refrigerator's crisper drawer. And cook these foods in as little water as needed. Steam or microwave foods without water if possible.

How to Use These Recipes

Weight Watchers® Miracle Foods: More Fruits, More Veggies gives you the nutrition facts you
need. To make your life easier, we've provided the following useful information with every recipe:

- A number calculated through **POINTS®** Food System, an integral part of the **Winning
  Points®** weight-loss program from Weight Watchers International, Inc.
- Diabetic exchange values for those who use them as a guide for planning meals
- A complete nutrient analysis per serving

POINTS Food System

Every recipe in the book includes a
number assigned through **POINTS** value. This
system uses a formula based on the
calorie, fat, and fiber content of the food.
Foods with more calories and fat (like
a slice of pepperoni pizza) receive high
numbers, while fruits and vegetables receive
low numbers. For more information about the
Winning Points weight-loss program and
the Weight Watchers meeting nearest you,
call 1-800-651-6000.

Diabetic Exchanges

Exchange values are provided for people who
use them for calorie-controlled diets and for
people with diabetes. All foods within a certain
group contain approximately the same amount
of nutrients and calories, so one serving of a
food from a food group can be substituted or
exchanged for one serving of any other item on
the list. The food groups are meat, starch,
vegetable, fruit, fat, and milk. The exchange
values are based on the Exchange Lists for

Meal Planning developed by the American
Diabetes Association and the American Dietetic
Association.

Nutritional Analyses

Each recipe has a complete list of nutrients;
numbers are based on these assumptions:

- Unless otherwise indicated, meat,
  poultry, and fish refer to skinned, boned,
  and cooked servings.
- When we give a range for an ingredient
  (3 to 3½ cups flour, for instance), we
  calculate using the lesser amount.
- Some alcohol calories evaporate during
  heating; the analysis reflects that.
- Only the amount of marinade absorbed
  by the food is used in calculation.
- Garnishes and optional ingredients are
  not included in analysis.

The nutritional values used in our calculations
either come from a computer program or are
provided by food manufacturers.

Appetizers
&
Beverages

Caribbean Fruits with Key Lime Dip photo, page 22

POINTS:

2

exchanges:

1½ Fruit

½ Skim Milk

per serving:

Calories 151

Carbohydrate 25.9g

Fat 1.3g (saturated 0.6g)

Fiber 2.9g

Protein 10.4g

Cholesterol 6mg

Sodium 329mg

Calcium 158mg

Iron 0.6mg

1   (8-ounce) carton key lime pie fat-free yogurt (such as Breyers)
1½ cups fat-free cream cheese
2   tablespoons powdered sugar
1   teaspoon coconut extract
1   cup mango cubes (about 1 medium mango)
1   cup fresh pineapple chunks or canned pineapple chunks in juice, drained
2   cups whole fresh strawberries
2   kiwifruit, peeled and cut into wedges
12 (6-inch) wooden skewers

1. Combine first 4 ingredients in a medium bowl; beat at medium speed of an electric mixer until smooth.

2. Thread fruit alternately onto each wooden skewer. Serve skewers with dip. Yield: 6 servings (serving size: 2 fruit skewers and about ⅓ cup dip).

quick tip: Stock the top shelf of your refrigerator with cut fresh fruit such as these skewers. Weight-loss winners say they are more likely to choose fruit over high-fat snack foods when it's visible and ready to eat.

Mixed Vegetables with Mexican Sour Cream Dip

1 cup reduced-fat sour cream

1½ tablespoons lime juice

1 tablespoon extra-virgin olive oil

2 tablespoons chopped fresh cilantro

½ teaspoon ground cumin

¼ teaspoon ground red pepper

¼ teaspoon salt

1 (8-ounce) cucumber, cut into 16 slices

1 (6-ounce) red bell pepper, cut into 16 strips

1 (8-ounce) squash, cut into 16 slices

POINTS:

2

exchanges:

½ Starch

½ Vegetable

1 Fat

per serving:

Calories 88

Carbohydrate 9.1g

Fat 4.4g (saturated 1.7g)

Fiber 1.4g

Protein 3.1g

Cholesterol 8mg

Sodium 146mg

Calcium 63mg

Iron 0.8mg

1. Combine first 7 ingredients in a small bowl; stir until well blended. Serve with cucumber, red bell pepper, and squash. Yield: 6 servings (serving size: about 3½ tablespoons dip and 8 vegetable pieces).

quick tip: For a variation, serve this spicy dip over a baked potato stuffed with plenty of steamed vegetables.

Eggplant and Kalamata Olive Spread

POINTS:
1

exchanges:
1½ Vegetable
½ Fat

per serving:
Calories 60
Carbohydrate 7.9g
Fat 2.4g (saturated 0.3g)
Fiber 2.3g
Protein 1.9g
Cholesterol 0mg
Sodium 278mg
Calcium 41mg
Iron 0.7mg

2	(1-pound) eggplants
2	teaspoons olive oil
2	large shallots, finely chopped
2	garlic cloves, minced
2	tablespoons sun-dried tomato paste (such as Amore)
½	teaspoon salt
¼	teaspoon pepper
½	cup plain fat-free yogurt
10	kalamata olives, pitted and chopped

1. Pierce eggplants several times with a fork, and microwave at HIGH 8 to 10 minutes or until tender. Cut in half, and let cool in refrigerator 5 minutes. Scrape the eggplant flesh into a medium bowl, discarding skin and seeds.

2. Heat olive oil in a large skillet over medium-high heat. Add shallots and garlic; cook, stirring constantly, 3 minutes. Add eggplant, tomato paste, salt, and pepper; cook 2 minutes, stirring often.

3. Transfer eggplant mixture to food processor bowl, and puree until smooth. Return eggplant mixture to a medium bowl; stir in yogurt and olives. Cover and chill 2 hours. Yield: 8 servings (serving size: ¼ cup).

quick tip: This Mediterranean-inspired appetizer is rich in heart-healthy monounsaturated fat, due to the kalamata olives and olive oil. Serve this hearty spread on toasted pita wedges or French bread rounds.

Tomatillo Guacamole photo, page 21

8	tomatillos
2	garlic cloves
1	jalapeño pepper, halved and seeded
1	avocado
1	tablespoon fresh lime juice
¼	cup tightly packed fresh cilantro
½	teaspoon salt

1. Discard husks and stems from tomatillos; wash thoroughly. Place tomatillos on an aluminum foil-lined baking sheet. Broil tomatillos 3 inches from heat 6 to 8 minutes or until tomatillos look blistered, turning once. Let cool.

2. Process garlic in food processor until garlic is minced. Add jalapeño pepper to garlic; process until minced, stopping once to scrape down sides.

3. Cut avocado in half, and remove seed; cut avocado into quarters, and peel. Add tomatillos, avocado, and remaining 3 ingredients to jalapeño pepper mixture. Process 15 seconds or until tomatillos are pureed. Cover and chill 1 hour. Yield: 5 servings (serving size: ¼ cup).

quick tip: Tomatillos resemble a small green tomato and are encased in a thin, parchment-like husk. Make sure to remove the husk before using. Tomatillos are rich in vitamin A, and contain a fair amount of vitamin C.

POINTS:
1

exchanges:
1 Vegetable
½ Fat

per serving:
Calories 50
Carbohydrate 5.0g
Fat 3.5g (saturated 0.6g)
Fiber 2.0g
Protein 1.0g
Cholesterol 0mg
Sodium 239mg
Calcium 12mg
Iron 0.7mg

Artichokes with Lemon Dipping Sauce

POINTS:

2

exchanges:

½ Starch
2 Vegetable
½ Fat

per serving:

Calories 104
Carbohydrate 17.7g
Fat 3.5g (saturated 0.1g)
Fiber 6.0g
Protein 3.2g
Cholesterol 3mg
Sodium 626mg
Calcium 60mg
Iron 1.9mg

¼ cup light mayonnaise-type salad dressing (such as Miracle Whip)
1   teaspoon grated lemon rind
¼ cup fresh lemon juice
1   tablespoon Dijon mustard
2   garlic cloves, minced
2   teaspoons salt
¼ teaspoon freshly ground pepper
4   medium artichokes

1. Combine first 7 ingredients in a small bowl; stir well. Cover and chill.

2. Wash artichokes by plunging up and down in cold water. Cut off stem ends; trim about ½ inch from top of each artichoke. Remove any loose bottom leaves. With scissors, trim one-fourth off top of each outer leaf.

3. Place artichokes in a large Dutch oven; add water to depth of 1 inch. Bring to a boil; cover, reduce heat, and simmer 25 minutes or until tender.

4. Serve artichokes with sauce. Yield: 4 servings (serving size: 1 artichoke and 2 tablespoons sauce).

cooking secret: You can reduce the prep time by cooking the artichokes in the microwave. Stand the artichokes in an 11- x 7-inch baking dish, and add 1 cup water to dish. Cover the dish with heavy-duty plastic wrap. Microwave at HIGH 15 to 20 minutes, giving the dish a quarter-turn halfway through the cooking time. Let stand 5 minutes. When the artichokes are done, the petal near the center will pull out easily.

Asian Lettuce Wraps

1   tablespoon plus 1 teaspoon reduced-fat chunky peanut butter

1½   teaspoons honey

1½   teaspoons cider vinegar

¼   teaspoon curry powder

1½   teaspoons low-sodium soy sauce

⅛   teaspoon ground red pepper

2   cups preshredded coleslaw mix

4   thin slices deli-style turkey breast

4   leaves iceberg lettuce or napa cabbage

POINTS:

2

exchanges:

½ Starch

½ Vegetable

1 Very Lean Meat

per serving:

Calories 85

Carbohydrate 7.5g

Fat 2.5g (saturated 0.6g)

Fiber 1.5g

Protein 9.2g

Cholesterol 16mg

Sodium 380mg

Calcium 25mg

Iron 0.8mg

1. Combine first 6 ingredients in a medium bowl; stir well. Add coleslaw mix; toss to coat.

2. Place one slice of turkey on each lettuce leaf; top with ½ cup coleslaw mixture. Roll up; secure each end with a wooden pick. Cut each wrap in half diagonally. Yield: 4 servings (serving size: 2 halves).

quick tip: Look for packages of preshredded coleslaw mix in your grocer's produce department to keep prep time to a minimum.

Broiled Lime and Soy Mushrooms

POINTS:
1

exchange:
1 Vegetable

per serving:
Calories 37
Carbohydrate 4.5g
Fat 1.8g (saturated 0.3g)
Fiber 1.1g
Protein 1.9g
Cholesterol 0mg
Sodium 165mg
Calcium 9mg
Iron 1.2mg

2 (8-ounce) packages fresh whole mushrooms
2 tablespoons lime juice
2 tablespoons low-sodium soy sauce
1½ teaspoons chopped fresh oregano
Cooking spray
2 teaspoons extra-virgin olive oil
¼ cup chopped fresh parsley

1. Wipe mushrooms clean with a damp cloth.

2. Combine mushrooms and next 3 ingredients in a large zip-top plastic bag. Seal; toss to coat well. Marinate in refrigerator 2 hours.

3. Place mushrooms on a baking sheet coated with cooking spray. Broil 5½ inches from heat 10 minutes.

4. Drizzle mushrooms with olive oil, and sprinkle with parsley. Serve warm. Yield: 6 servings.

cooking secret: Clean mushrooms by either wiping them with a damp cloth or, if necessary, rinsing them with cold water and drying thoroughly. Fresh mushrooms should never be soaked because they absorb water and will become mushy.

Roasted Red Pepper and Ripe Olive Crostini photo, page 23

16   (¼-inch thick) slices diagonally cut French baguette
Cooking spray
1   tablespoon dried basil, divided
1   (4¼-ounce) can chopped ripe olives, drained
1½ tablespoons red wine vinegar
½   teaspoon minced garlic (about ½ clove)
¼   cup (1 ounce) crumbled feta cheese with basil and tomato
1   (15-ounce) jar roasted red peppers, drained and finely chopped

POINTS:

1

exchange:

½ Starch

per serving:

Calories 45
Carbohydrate 5.6g
Fat 1.5g (saturated 0.5g)
Fiber 0.5g
Protein 1.1g
Cholesterol 1mg
Sodium 223mg
Calcium 23mg
Iron 0.5mg

1. Place bread slices on a baking sheet; coat with cooking spray, and sprinkle evenly with 1½ teaspoons basil. Bake at 350° for 15 minutes or until golden and crispy. Remove bread slices from baking sheet to a wire rack; let cool completely.

2. Combine olives, remaining basil, vinegar, and garlic in a small bowl; gently stir in cheese and peppers. Let stand 15 minutes.

3. Spoon 2 tablespoons olive mixture onto each bread slice. Yield: 16 servings (serving size: 1 crostini).

quick tip: This easy appetizer can be prepared ahead of time. Assemble the red pepper-olive mixture, cover it with plastic wrap, and store it in the refrigerator for up to 8 hours. Then, spoon the mixture on the baguette slices before guests arrive.

Strawberry Malt

POINTS:

4

exchanges:

1 Starch

½ Fruit

1 Skim Milk

per serving:

Calories 211

Carbohydrate 39.0g

Fat 3.0g (saturated 1.5g)

Fiber 2.1g

Protein 8.5g

Cholesterol 9mg

Sodium 142mg

Calcium 277mg

Iron 0.9mg

1   cup frozen unsweetened whole strawberries, partially thawed
½   cup low-fat vanilla ice cream
½   cup fat-free milk
1   tablespoon malted milk powder

1. Combine all ingredients in container of an electric blender. Cover and process until smooth, stopping once to scrape down sides. Serve immediately. Yield: 1 serving.

super food: This sweet strawberry malt is perfect for a snack or dessert. It's also loaded with calcium, which is essential for strong bones and teeth. One serving satisfies about one-third of your daily calcium quota.

Tomatillo Guacamole
recipe, page 15

**Caribbean Fruits with
Key Lime Dip**
recipe, page 12

Roasted Red Pepper and
Ripe Olive Crostini
recipe, page 19

Chocolate-Banana Smoothie photo, facing page

1   cup frozen sliced banana (about 1 large)
2   cups 1% low-fat chocolate milk
⅔   cup fat-free, no-sugar-added chocolate fudge ice cream
    (such as Edy's)
Chocolate shavings (optional)

POINTS:

4

exchanges:

1 Starch
1 Fruit
1 Skim Milk

1. Combine first 3 ingredients in container of an electric blender. Cover and process until smooth, stopping once to scrape down sides. Garnish with chocolate shavings, if desired, and serve immediately. Yield: 3 servings (serving size: about 1 cup).

quick tip: This smoothie is a great use for overripe bananas, which are extra sweet. Simply slice the overripe banana, and store it in a freezer-safe plastic bag. Then, you'll have the beginnings of a delicious and nutritious snack.

per serving:

Calories 204
Carbohydrate 40.8g
Fat 1.9g (saturated 1.1g)
Fiber 1.6g
Protein 7.6g
Cholesterol 7mg
Sodium 147mg
Calcium 205mg
Iron 0.7mg

Tropical Peach Punch

POINTS:

3

exchanges:

½ Starch

2½ Fruit

per serving:

Calories 190

Carbohydrate 47.1g

Fat 0.1g (saturated 0.0g)

Fiber 2.4g

Protein 1.2g

Cholesterol 0mg

Sodium 41mg

Calcium 6mg

Iron 0.1mg

2   cups coarsely chopped peeled fresh peaches (about 4 peaches)

1½ cups orange-pineapple juice

½   cup frozen white grape juice concentrate

2   cups sugar-free ginger ale

1. Combine first 3 ingredients in container of an electric blender; cover and process until smooth, stopping once to scrape down sides.

2. Fill 4 tall glasses with crushed ice; add 1 cup juice mixture and ½ cup ginger ale to each glass. Stir gently; serve immediately. Yield: 4 servings.

quick tip: The juice mixture can easily be made a day in advance. Cover and store it in the refrigerator, and add the ginger ale at serving time.

Cranberry-Citrus Spritzer

2¾ cups cranberry juice cocktail, chilled
¾ cup citrus punch, chilled (such as Minute Maid)
2½ cups sugar-free lemon-lime soda, chilled

1. Combine all ingredients in a large bowl; stir well. Serve immediately.
Yield: 6 servings (serving size: 1 cup).

super food: While fruit juices aren't rich in fiber like whole fruits, they are good sources of other nutrients. Cranberry juice cocktail, for example, is a great source of vitamin C, and counts toward your daily water quota.

POINTS:
2

exchanges:
½ Starch
1 Fruit

per serving:
Calories 79
Carbohydrate 19.6g
Fat 0.0g (saturated 0.0g)
Fiber 0.0g
Protein 0.0g
Cholesterol 0mg
Sodium 29mg
Calcium 13mg
Iron 0.2mg

Warm Rosemary Lemonade Sipper

POINTS:

2

exchanges:

1½ Starch

3⅔ cups water

⅓   cup fresh lemon juice

½   cup sugar

1   teaspoon minced fresh rosemary

Fresh rosemary sprigs (optional)

per serving:

Calories 102

Carbohydrate 26.7g

Fat 0.0g (saturated 0.0g)

Fiber 0.1g

Protein 0.1g

Cholesterol 0mg

Sodium 7mg

Calcium 6mg

Iron 0.0mg

1. Combine first 4 ingredients in a medium saucepan. Bring mixture to a boil, stirring until sugar dissolves. Remove from heat; let stand 10 minutes. Strain mixture, discarding rosemary. Serve warm or chilled with fresh rosemary sprigs, if desired. Yield: 4 servings (serving size: 1 cup).

quick tip: Like all citrus fruits, lemons are bursting with vitamin C. Preserve that antioxidant vitamin by storing fresh lemons in the refrigerator.

Desserts

Citrusy Melon and Strawberry Cup

POINTS:
1

exchanges:
1½ Fruit

per serving:
Calories 86
Carbohydrate 21.2g
Fat 0.4g (saturated 0.1g)
Fiber 1.8g
Protein 1.3g
Cholesterol 0mg
Sodium 11mg
Calcium 20mg
Iron 0.4mg

1 tablespoon sugar
1 tablespoon lemon juice
3 tablespoons frozen orange juice concentrate, thawed
1½ cups bite-size fresh cantaloupe chunks
1½ cups bite-size fresh honeydew melon chunks
1 cup halved fresh strawberries

1. Combine first 3 ingredients in a large bowl; stir well. Add remaining ingredients; stir gently. Yield: 4 servings (serving size: 1 cup).

 quick tip: This simple dessert shows off several of the most nutrient-packed fruits. Cantaloupe is the most nutritious of all melons, while a cup of strawberries has more fiber than a slice of whole-wheat bread.
Keep prep time to a minimum by picking up precut fruit from your grocer's produce or deli department.

Pear and Cranberry Compote

¼   cup water
½   teaspoon grated lemon rind
1   teaspoon fresh lemon juice
⅓   cup sugar
4   small pears, peeled, cored, and cut into fourths
1   cup fresh cranberries

1. Combine first 4 ingredients in a medium saucepan; bring to a boil. Reduce heat, and simmer, uncovered, 5 minutes or until slightly thickened, stirring occasionally.

2. Add pear and cranberries; stir gently. Bring to a boil. Cover, reduce heat, and simmer 5 minutes or until cranberries pop. Pour mixture into a medium-size bowl. Cover and chill 30 minutes. Serve chilled. Yield: 4 servings (serving size: 1 cup).

quick tip: You'll know a pear is ripe by applying gentle pressure at the base of the stem. If it yields slightly to pressure, it's ripe.

POINTS:

3

exchanges:

1 Starch
2 Fruit

per serving:

Calories 172
Carbohydrate 44.2g
Fat 0.7g (saturated 0.0g)
Fiber 4.2g
Protein 0.7g
Cholesterol 0mg
Sodium 0mg
Calcium 20mg
Iron 0.5mg

Watermelon and Blackberries with Lemon Syrup photo, page 43

POINTS:
1

exchanges:
½ Starch
1 Fruit

per serving:
Calories 108
Carbohydrate 26.4g
Fat 0.7g (saturated 0.1g)
Fiber 3.7g
Protein 1.2g
Cholesterol 0mg
Sodium 3mg
Calcium 29mg
Iron 0.5mg

½ cup water
¼ cup sugar
½ teaspoon grated lemon rind
1 tablespoon fresh lemon juice
4 cups seeded watermelon balls
2 cups fresh blackberries

1. Combine first 4 ingredients in a small saucepan; stir well. Bring mixture to a boil over medium-high heat; cook 45 seconds or until sugar dissolves. Remove from heat; cover and chill 30 minutes.

2. Combine watermelon and blackberries in a large bowl; add lemon syrup, and toss gently. Yield: 5 servings (serving size: 1 cup).

 super food: You'll find this easy dessert filling because it's rich in fiber, thanks to the blackberries. Blackberries contain more fiber than any other berry. One cup of blackberries packs 40% more fiber than a bowl of shredded-wheat cereal.

Macerated Raspberries with Nectarines

1   cup dry red wine
⅓   cup sugar
8   whole cloves
2   (3-inch) cinnamon sticks
2   cups fresh or frozen raspberries, thawed
½   teaspoon vanilla extract
3   cups sliced unpeeled fresh nectarine (about 4 nectarines)

1. Combine first 4 ingredients in a small saucepan. Bring to a boil over high heat; cook, uncovered, 8 to 10 minutes until sauce is reduced to ⅓ cup. Remove from heat. Place raspberries in a medium bowl. Pour sauce through a wire-mesh strainer over berries; let stand, uncovered, 30 minutes or until cool. Stir in vanilla.

2. To serve, place ¾ cup nectarine slices in each of 4 dessert dishes; spoon ¼ cup raspberry mixture over each serving. Yield: 4 servings.

POINTS:

2

exchanges:

1 Starch

1½ Fruit

per serving:

Calories 158

Carbohydrate 38.7g

Fat 0.9g (saturated 0.1g)

Fiber 6.5g

Protein 1.6g

Cholesterol 0mg

Sodium 5mg

Calcium 23mg

Iron 0.8mg

cooking secret: Macerating is similar to marinating. A food, usually fruit, is soaked in a liquid such as wine, liquor, or a flavorful syrup to infuse that food with more flavor.

Baked Plums with Orange Custard Sauce

POINTS:

3

exchanges:

1 Starch
1 Fruit
½ Fat

per serving:

Calories 155
Carbohydrate 30.6g
Fat 2.5g (saturated 0.8g)
Fiber 1.3g
Protein 3.7g
Cholesterol 57mg
Sodium 39mg
Calcium 66mg
Iron 0.4mg

Orange Custard Sauce
5   red plums, quartered and pitted
Cooking spray
3   tablespoons sugar
¼   cup unsweetened apple juice

1. Prepare Orange Custard Sauce.

2. Place plums in a 9-inch pieplate coated with cooking spray. Sprinkle with sugar. Pour apple juice over plums. Bake at 400° for 18 to 20 minutes or just until plums are tender. Let cool slightly.

3. Spoon warm plums and juice evenly into individual dessert dishes. Top with Orange Custard Sauce. Yield: 4 servings (serving size: 5 plum quarters and juice, and 3 tablespoons sauce).

Orange Custard Sauce

1   large egg
2   tablespoons sugar
¾   cup 1% low-fat milk
1   teaspoon grated orange rind
½   teaspoon vanilla extract

1. Combine egg and sugar in a medium saucepan, beating well with a whisk. Add milk. Cook over low heat, stirring constantly, about 15 minutes or until thickened. Remove from heat, and stir in orange rind and vanilla. Pour into a small bowl; cover and chill 30 minutes. Yield: ¾ cup (serving size: 3 tablespoons). Calories: 66; **POINTS:** 1.

Peach Sundaes with Blueberry Sauce

Blueberry Sauce

1 cup cubed peeled fresh peaches (about 2 peaches)

1⅓ cups low-fat vanilla ice cream

1. Prepare Blueberry Sauce.

2. Place ¼ cup peaches in each of 4 dessert dishes; top each with ⅓ cup ice cream and ¼ cup Blueberry Sauce. Serve immediately. Yield: 4 servings.

Blueberry Sauce

3 tablespoons sugar

1½ teaspoons cornstarch

½ cup water

1 cup fresh blueberries

1. Combine sugar and cornstarch in a small saucepan; gradually stir in water. Bring mixture to a boil over medium-high heat, stirring constantly. Add blueberries, and cook 4 minutes or until mixture boils in center, stirring often. Reduce heat to medium, and cook 2 minutes, stirring often; cool slightly. Yield: 1 cup (serving size: ¼ cup). Calories: 60; **POINTS:** 1.

 quick tip: This versatile blueberry sauce also can be served over waffles, angel food cake, or pancakes.

POINTS:

3

exchanges:

1½ Starch

1½ Fruit

per serving:

Calories 145

Carbohydrate 32.0g

Fat 1.5g (saturated 1.0g)

Fiber 2.5g

Protein 2.5g

Cholesterol 7mg

Sodium 6mg

Calcium 71mg

Iron 0.1mg

Gingered Grapefruit Sorbet photo, page 2

POINTS:

3

exchanges:

1 Starch

2 Fruit

1   (1-pound) package frozen melon, peach, and strawberry mixture

2   cups red grapefruit juice (such as Ocean Spray)

½   cup honey

1   tablespoon lemon juice

1   tablespoon grated fresh ginger

per serving:

Calories 158

Carbohydrate 45.1g

Fat 0.1g (saturated 0.0g)

Fiber 1.1g

Protein 0.7g

Cholesterol 0mg

Sodium 18mg

Calcium 3mg

Iron 0.9mg

1. Combine all ingredients in a large bowl; stir well. Pour one-third of mixture into an electric blender; cover and process until smooth, stopping once to scrape down sides. Pour mixture into a 13- x 9-inch pan. Repeat procedure in 2 batches with remaining mixture. Cover and freeze at least 8 hours or until firm.

2. Remove mixture from freezer, and let stand 10 minutes. Serve immediately, or spoon into an airtight freezer-safe container; cover and freeze for up to 1 month. Yield: 6 servings (serving size: 1 cup).

quick tip: Frozen fruits and vegetables are just as nutritious as their fresh counterparts because they are harvested and frozen at their peak. Stock up on frozen fruits such as the mixture in this flavorful sorbet so that you can enjoy fruit desserts year-round.

Minted Watermelon Granita photo, page 2

⅓   cup sugar

⅓   cup watermelon juice or water

6   cups seeded watermelon cubes

¼   cup lime juice

½   teaspoon peppermint extract

2   teaspoons chopped fresh mint

1. Combine sugar and watermelon juice in a small saucepan; bring to a boil. Cook, stirring constantly, until sugar dissolves.

2. Place watermelon cubes, lime juice, and peppermint in container of an electric blender; cover and process until smooth, stopping once to scrape down sides. Add sugar mixture; cover and process until blended. Pour mixture into a 13- x 9-inch pan; cover and freeze at least 8 hours or until firm.

3. Remove mixture from freezer, and scrape entire mixture with tines of a fork until fluffy. Toss mint into granita; serve immediately. Yield: 6 servings (serving size: 1 cup).

cooking secret: The granita may be frozen in an airtight freezer-safe container for up to 1 month.

POINTS:

2

exchanges:

½ Starch

1 Fruit

per serving:

Calories 98

Carbohydrate 23.4g

Fat 0.7g (saturated 0.1g)

Fiber 0.8g

Protein 1.0g

Cholesterol 0mg

Sodium 3mg

Calcium 14mg

Iron 0.3mg

Pineapple-Mint Ice photo, page 2

POINTS:

2

exchanges:

2 Fruit

per serving:

Calories 117
Carbohydrate 28.9g
Fat 0.0g (saturated 0.0g)
Fiber 1.4g
Protein 0.0g
Cholesterol 0mg
Sodium 2mg
Calcium 20mg
Iron 0.6mg

1   (20-ounce) can pineapple chunks in juice, chilled and undrained
2   tablespoons coarsely chopped fresh mint
Fresh mint sprigs (optional)

1. Set aside 3 pineapple chunks for garnish. Place remaining pineapple and juice into an 8-inch square pan. Cover and freeze 1½ to 2 hours or until almost frozen.

2. Process frozen pineapple and chopped mint in a food processor until smooth, but not melted. Serve immediately; garnish with reserved pineapple chunks and mint sprigs, if desired. Yield: 3 servings (serving size: ¾ cup).

quick tip: This simple dessert is an easy way toward your five fruits or vegetables a day. One serving counts as two fruits. You can substitute any canned fruit packed in its own juice.

Peach Ice Cream

1   (1-pound) package frozen peaches
1½ cups sliced ripe banana (about 2 medium)
1   cup low-fat vanilla ice cream
½   cup frozen orange juice concentrate, thawed
¼   cup sifted powdered sugar
¾   to 1 teaspoon coconut extract

1. Add all ingredients to food processor bowl; process until smooth.
Serve immediately, or freeze, covered, in an airtight freezer-safe
container until ready to serve. Yield: 6 servings (serving size: ¾ cup).

 meal idea: Serve this easy ice cream with Spicy Catfish
Fingers and Cole Slaw (page 56).

POINTS:

3

exchanges:

1 Starch

1½ Fruit

per serving:

Calories 160
Carbohydrate 37.0g
Fat 0.9g (saturated 0.6g)
Fiber 2.6g
Protein 2.5g
Cholesterol 3mg
Sodium 3mg
Calcium 44mg
Iron 0.2mg

Double Berry-Brownie Dessert <small>photo, facing page</small>

POINTS:

5

exchanges:

3 Starch

1 Fruit

½ Fat

3 tablespoons seedless strawberry jam, melted
1½ tablespoons water
1 cup fresh raspberries
1 cup sliced fresh strawberries
4 low-fat chocolate brownies
¾ cup frozen fat-free whipped topping, thawed
¼ cup fat-free fudge ice cream topping

per serving:

Calories 268

Carbohydrate 59.7g

Fat 2.8g (saturated 1.0g)

Fiber 4.0g

Protein 1.5g

Cholesterol 0mg

Sodium 141mg

Calcium 23mg

Iron 1.6mg

1. Combine jam and water in a medium bowl; stir in raspberries and strawberries. Reserve 2 tablespoons berry mixture for topping. Tear brownies into small pieces, reserving several pieces for topping.

2. Place several brownie pieces in each of 4 dessert cups. Spoon about ¼ cup berry mixture over brownie. Repeat layers. Top each with whipped topping, ice cream topping, reserved berry mixture, and reserved brownie pieces. Yield: 4 servings (serving size: 1 brownie, ½ cup berry mixture, 3 tablespoons whipped topping, and 1 tablespoon ice cream topping).

Peach-Almond Tart
recipe, page 49

**Watermelon and Blackberries
with Lemon Syrup**
recipe, page 32

43

Chocolate-Banana Ice Cream Pie photo, facing page

2   tablespoons fat-free caramel-flavored sundae syrup
2   cups fat-free frozen whipped topping, thawed
4   cups fat-free vanilla ice cream, softened
1   (6-ounce) ready-made chocolate crumb piecrust
¼   cup plus 2 teaspoons fat-free chocolate-flavored sundae syrup, divided
4   cups sliced banana (about 5 medium)
2   tablespoons chopped dry roasted unsalted peanuts

POINTS:
7

exchanges:
3 Starch
1 Fruit
1 Fat

per serving:
Calories 352
Carbohydrate 63.1g
Fat 6.9g (saturated 1.4g)
Fiber 2.3g
Protein 4.5g
Cholesterol 0mg
Sodium 176mg
Calcium 95mg
Iron 0.8mg

1. Combine caramel syrup and whipped topping in a medium bowl; gently fold 3 times to form swirls.

2. Spoon ice cream into piecrust. Drizzle 2 tablespoons chocolate syrup over ice cream. Spread whipped topping mixture over chocolate syrup. Cover and freeze 2 hours or until firm.

3. Cut pie into 8 pieces. Place on individual serving dishes. Top each piece with ½ cup banana, 1 teaspoon chocolate syrup, and 1 teaspoon peanuts. Yield: 8 servings.

quick tip: If you're in the mood for strawberries, simply substitute 4 cups sliced fresh strawberries for the bananas. Top off the strawberries with 2 tablespoons toasted slivered almonds instead of the peanuts.

Fresh Strawberry-Lime Pie

POINTS:

3

exchanges:

1 Starch

½ Fruit

1 Fat

per serving:

Calories 167

Carbohydrate 25.7g

Fat 5.3g (saturated 1.0g)

Fiber 1.7g

Protein 2.3g

Cholesterol 0mg

Sodium 112mg

Calcium 11mg

Iron 0.7mg

1   (0.3-ounce) package sugar-free strawberry-flavored gelatin
⅔   cup boiling water
4   cups quartered fresh strawberries
1½ tablespoons fresh lime juice, divided
1   (6-ounce) ready-made shortbread piecrust (such as Keebler)
2   cups fat-free frozen whipped topping, thawed
¼   teaspoon grated lime rind

1. Combine gelatin and boiling water in a medium bowl; stir until gelatin dissolves. Cover and freeze 8 minutes or until consistency of unbeaten egg white. Add strawberries and 1 tablespoon lime juice; stir well. Spoon into crust; cover and chill 2 hours or until firm.

2. Combine whipped topping and remaining ½ tablespoon lime juice in a small bowl.

3. Cut pie into 8 pieces. Place on individual serving dishes. Top each piece with ¼ cup whipped topping mixture; sprinkle each with grated lime rind. Serve immediately. Yield: 8 servings.

 cooking secret: For the freshest flavor, stir together the whipped topping and lime juice just before serving.

Rhubarb-Strawberry Pie

3   cups sliced fresh rhubarb

2   cups sliced fresh strawberries

1   cup sugar

⅓   cup all-purpose flour

1   teaspoon vanilla extract

½   teaspoon ground cinnamon

Cooking spray

½   (15-ounce) package refrigerated piecrusts

POINTS:

6

exchanges:

2½ Starch

½ Fruit

1½ Fat

per serving:

Calories 260

Carbohydrate 46.9g

Fat 7.4g (saturated 3.1g)

Fiber 1.3g

Protein 1.7g

Cholesterol 5mg

Sodium 103mg

Calcium 48mg

Iron 0.6mg

1. Combine first 6 ingredients in a large bowl; toss gently to coat. Spoon mixture into a 9-inch deep-dish pieplate coated with cooking spray.

2. Unfold piecrust, and place on a lightly floured surface. Roll piecrust lightly to press out fold lines. Place on top of fruit; fold edges under, and crimp. Using a sharp knife, cut 4 (1-inch) slits in top of piecrust to allow steam to escape. Place pieplate on a baking sheet. Bake at 400° for 50 minutes or until crust is golden. Transfer pie to a wire rack; cool completely. Yield: 8 servings.

quick tip: This simple pie is similar to a cobbler, so spoon it into dessert dishes for serving. Make it in early spring or summer when fresh rhubarb is at its prime.

Glazed Fruit Tart with Coconut Crust

POINTS:

4

exchanges:

2 Starch

½ Fruit

1 Fat

per serving:

Calories 199

Carbohydrate 36.6g

Fat 5.8g (saturated 4.6g)

Fiber 4.3g

Protein 3.0g

Cholesterol 0mg

Sodium 53mg

Calcium 20mg

Iron 0.9mg

2   large egg whites

2   teaspoons brown sugar

1½ cups crushed bite-size shredded whole wheat cereal biscuits
     (about 1 cup whole biscuits)

1¼ cups flaked sweetened coconut

Cooking spray

2   kiwifruit, peeled and sliced crosswise

½   cup apricot all-fruit spread

2   cups sliced unpeeled fresh nectarine (about 3 nectarines)

2   cups sliced fresh strawberries

1. Combine egg whites and brown sugar in a small bowl, stirring well.
Stir in cereal and coconut; fluff with a fork until thoroughly coated.
Lightly press cereal mixture in bottom and ½ inch up sides of a 10-
inch springform pan coated with cooking spray.

2. Bake at 350° for 15 minutes or until edges begin to brown. Cool
completely.

3. Remove sides of pan, and place crust on a serving plate. Arrange
kiwifruit around outer edge of crust. Place fruit spread in a large bowl;
stir until smooth. Add nectarines and strawberries; stir gently until fruit
is thoroughly coated. Mound fruit in center of tart, and arrange attrac-
tively. Cut tart into wedges, and serve immediately. Yield: 8 servings.

 super food: Using shredded whole wheat cereal biscuits for
the crust of this easy-yet-elegant fruit tart increases the
fiber content.

Peach-Almond Tart photo, page 42

½ (15-ounce) package refrigerated piecrusts
Cooking spray
4 cups sliced peeled fresh or frozen peaches (about 8 peaches)
¼ cup finely chopped dried apricots
3 tablespoons granulated sugar
1 tablespoon plus 1 teaspoon cornstarch
1 tablespoon turbinado or granulated sugar
2 tablespoons sliced almonds

POINTS:

4

exchanges:
1 Starch
1 Fruit
1½ Fat

per serving:
Calories 210
Carbohydrate 33.9g
Fat 8.0g (saturated 3.1g)
Fiber 2.4g
Protein 1.6g
Cholesterol 5mg
Sodium 101mg
Calcium 11mg
Iron 0.4mg

1. Unfold piecrust, and place on a lightly floured surface. Roll piecrust into a 12-inch circle. Place on a baking sheet or pizza pan coated with cooking spray.

2. Combine peaches, apricots, granulated sugar, and cornstarch; toss gently. Spread mixture over piecrust, leaving a 2-inch border. Fold a 2-inch border over fruit, pressing to gently seal where piecrust overlaps (piecrust will partially cover fruit). Coat edges lightly with cooking spray, and sprinkle with turbinado sugar. Sprinkle almonds over peach mixture.

3. Bake at 425° for 22 minutes or until pastry is lightly browned. Let cool on baking sheet on a wire rack 30 minutes. Yield: 8 servings.

 super food: The deep yellow-orange color of peaches and apricots indicates these fruits are rich in the cancer-fighting antioxidant beta-carotene. Look for fresh peaches with a gold or yellow skin, which is the true sign of a ripe peach.

Apple-Cherry Cobbler

POINTS:

4

exchanges:

2 Starch

½ Fruit

1 Fat

per serving:

Calories 216

Carbohydrate 40.3g

Fat 5.2g (saturated 2.8g)

Fiber 1.9g

Protein 3.0g

Cholesterol 59mg

Sodium 160mg

Calcium 56mg

Iron 1.0mg

1   (14.5-ounce) can pitted red tart cherries in water, drained
3½ cups cubed, peeled Braeburn apple (about 3 large apples)
¼   cup granulated sugar
¾   cup all-purpose flour
1¼ teaspoons baking powder
⅛   teaspoon salt
3   tablespoons butter or stick margarine, melted
⅔   cup sugar
2   large eggs
½   teaspoon vanilla extract
¼   teaspoon almond extract
1   teaspoon powdered sugar (optional)

1. Combine first 3 ingredients in a large bowl; stir gently. Spoon into a 9-inch square pan.

2. Combine flour, baking powder, and salt in a small bowl; set aside. Combine butter and next 4 ingredients in a large bowl; stir well. Add flour mixture, and stir well. Pour batter over fruit. Bake at 350° for 40 minutes or until golden and a wooden pick inserted in center comes out clean. Sprinkle powdered sugar over cobbler before serving, if desired. Serve warm. Yield: 9 servings (serving size: about ½ cup).

 quick tip: Choose apples that have good color and smooth skin without bruises. For cooking or baking, select Braeburn, Rome, McIntosh, or the all-purpose Golden Delicious.

Apple-Cranberry Crisp

⅓   cup all-purpose flour

¼   cup plus 1 tablespoon granulated sugar, divided

¼   cup firmly packed brown sugar

¼   cup butter or stick margarine, cut into small pieces

7   cups sliced, peeled Golden Delicious apple (about 6 large apples)

¼   cup sweetened dried cranberries

½   teaspoon ground ginger

Cooking spray

POINTS:

4

exchanges:

1½ Starch

1 Fruit

1 Fat

per serving:

Calories 189

Carbohydrate 34.5g

Fat 6.2g (saturated 3.7g)

Fiber 2.2g

Protein 0.7g

Cholesterol 16mg

Sodium 62mg

Calcium 12mg

Iron 0.5mg

1. Combine flour, ¼ cup granulated sugar, and brown sugar in a small bowl; cut in butter with a pastry blender until mixture is crumbly.

2. Combine apple, cranberries, ginger, and remaining 1 tablespoon granulated sugar in a large bowl; stir gently. Spoon fruit mixture into an 8-inch square pan coated with cooking spray, and sprinkle with crumb mixture. Bake at 400° for 35 minutes or until golden. Serve warm. Yield: 8 servings (serving size: about ½ cup).

super food: Apples are a delicious addition to simple desserts such as this crisp. They also are loaded with fiber and may help prevent lung disease, as recent research suggests.

Nectarine Betty

POINTS:

5

exchanges:

2½ Starch

1 Fruit

1 Fat

per serving:

Calories 266

Carbohydrate 52.1g

Fat 7.2g (saturated 3.2g)

Fiber 3.4g

Protein 3.2g

Cholesterol 13mg

Sodium 147mg

Calcium 19mg

Iron 1.1mg

5   cups thinly sliced unpeeled nectarine (about 6 nectarines)
½   cup sugar
2   tablespoons raisins
2   tablespoons unsweetened apple juice
2   (1-ounce) slices white bread
4   soft oatmeal cookies (such as Archway)
2   tablespoons butter or stick margarine, melted
Cooking spray

1. Combine first 4 ingredients in a large bowl; mix gently. Set aside.

2. Add bread slices to food processor bowl; process until crumbs are fine. Remove breadcrumbs from processor bowl; set aside. Place cookies in processor bowl; pulse 8 times or until crumbs are coarse.

3. Combine cookie crumbs, breadcrumbs, and butter in a medium bowl; toss with a fork. Sprinkle ½ cup crumb mixture in bottom of 1½-quart casserole or soufflé dish coated with cooking spray. Top with half of nectarine mixture; sprinkle with ¾ cup crumb mixture, and top with remaining nectarine mixture. Sprinkle with remaining crumb mixture.

4. Cover and bake at 350° for 35 minutes or until fruit is tender. Uncover and bake 15 additional minutes or until bubbly. Serve warm. Yield: 6 servings (serving size: ⅔ cup).

 quick tip: A betty is a fruit dessert topped with a buttered breadcrumb mixture that has been baked until golden.

Blueberry Streusel Cake

¼   cup butter or stick margarine
⅔   cup sugar
1   large egg
1¼ cups all-purpose flour
1¼ teaspoons baking powder
⅛   teaspoon salt
½   cup 1% low-fat milk
1   teaspoon vanilla extract
Cooking spray
1½ cups fresh blueberries
Streusel Topping

POINTS:

6

exchanges:

2½ Starch
½ Fruit
2 Fat

per serving:

Calories 271
Carbohydrate 43.3g
Fat 9.4g (saturated 5.3g)
Fiber 1.4g
Protein 3.9g
Cholesterol 50mg
Sodium 211mg
Calcium 73mg
Iron 1.4mg

1. In a large bowl, beat butter at medium speed of an electric mixer until creamy; gradually add sugar, beating well. Add egg, beating well.

2. Combine flour, baking powder, and salt in a small bowl; add to butter mixture alternately with milk, beginning and ending with flour mixture. Mix at low speed after each addition until blended. Stir in vanilla. Pour batter into a 9-inch round cakepan coated with cooking spray. Sprinkle blueberries over top of batter. Sprinkle Streusel Topping over blueberries.

3. Bake at 350° for 45 to 47 minutes or until a wooden pick inserted in center comes out clean. Cool in pan on a wire rack. Cut into wedges to serve. Yield: 8 servings.

Streusel Topping

3   tablespoons sugar
3   tablespoons all-purpose flour
½   teaspoon ground cinnamon
1½ tablespoons butter or stick margarine, cut into small pieces

1. Combine first 3 ingredients in a medium bowl; cut in butter with a pastry blender until mixture resembles coarse meal. Yield: ½ cup.

Pear Upside-Down Banana Cake

POINTS:

6

exchanges:

2½ Starch

½ Fruit

1½ Fat

per serving:

Calories 273

Carbohydrate 47.5g

Fat 8.4g (saturated 4.8g)

Fiber 1.8g

Protein 3.5g

Cholesterol 47mg

Sodium 242mg

Calcium 28mg

Iron 1.3mg

1   tablespoon butter or stick margarine, melted
¼   cup firmly packed brown sugar
2   cups thinly sliced peeled red pear (about 1½ small pears)
¼   cup butter or stick margarine, softened
⅔   cup granulated sugar
1   large egg
½   cup mashed ripe banana (about 1 medium)
1¼ cups all-purpose flour
¾   teaspoon baking soda
⅛   teaspoon salt
¼   cup low-fat buttermilk

1. Coat bottom of a 9-inch round cakepan with melted butter. Sprinkle with brown sugar, and arrange pear slices over sugar in an overlapping pattern.

2. Beat ¼ cup butter at medium speed of an electric mixer until creamy; gradually add ⅔ cup granulated sugar, beating well. Add egg and banana, beating well.

3. Combine flour, soda, and salt in a small bowl; add to butter mixture alternately with buttermilk, beginning and ending with flour mixture. Mix at low speed after each addition until blended. Spoon batter over pear slices.

4. Bake at 350° for 30 to 35 minutes or until a wooden pick inserted in center comes out clean. Cool 5 minutes in pan on a wire rack. Loosen cake from sides of pan with a narrow metal spatula and invert onto a cake plate. Serve warm. Yield: 8 servings.

 cooking secret: An overripe banana lends an extra sweet taste to this cake. When the banana peel turns black, the banana's flavor is intensified, and the banana is easier to mash.

Fish
&
Shellfish

Spicy Catfish Fingers with Cucumber Coleslaw

POINTS:

6

exchanges:

1 Starch

1½ Vegetable

2½ Lean Meat

1 Fat

per serving:

Calories 291

Carbohydrate 23.0g

Fat 12.2g (saturated 2.2g)

Fiber 2.7g

Protein 22.6g

Cholesterol 91mg

Sodium 1323mg

Calcium 91mg

Iron 2.1mg

¼   cup crushed corn flakes cereal
1½ tablespoons yellow cornmeal
2½ teaspoons Creole seasoning
1   pound catfish fillets, cut crosswise into 12 strips
Cooking spray
Cucumber Coleslaw

1. Combine first 3 ingredients in a shallow dish. Lightly coat catfish with cooking spray. Dredge catfish in cereal mixture. Place catfish in a jellyroll pan coated with cooking spray. Lightly coat catfish again with cooking spray.

2. Bake, uncovered, at 425° for 10 to 12 minutes or until fish flakes easily when tested with a fork. Serve with Cucumber Coleslaw. Yield: 4 servings (serving size: 3 catfish fingers and 1½ cups coleslaw).

Cucumber Coleslaw

1   (11.5-ounce) package country-style fresh slaw mix (about 5 cups)
1   cup thinly sliced cucumber (about 1 small)
½   cup reduced-calorie coleslaw dressing (such as Marzetti's Lite Slaw Dressing)

1. Combine all ingredients; mix well. Yield: 4 servings (serving size: 1½ cups). Calories: 124; ***POINTS:*** 3.

meal idea: Round out the meal with Peach Ice Cream (page 39).

Grouper with Mild Chipotle Sauce

½ to 1 chipotle chile pepper in adobo sauce, drained, seeded, and
      mashed
1   (8-ounce) can tomato sauce
½   teaspoon orange rind
⅓   cup fresh orange juice
½   cup fat-free evaporated milk
1½ teaspoons butter
½   teaspoon ground cumin
¼   teaspoon salt
⅛   teaspoon pepper
1   tablespoon butter
4   (6-ounce) grouper fillets
Orange slices (optional)

POINTS:
5

exchanges:
½ Starch
1 Vegetable
5 Very Lean Meat

per serving:
Calories 251
Carbohydrate 11.0g
Fat 6.4g (saturated 3.2g)
Fiber 1.0g
Protein 36.0g
Cholesterol 76mg
Sodium 694mg
Calcium 155mg
Iron 2.2mg

1. Heat a large nonstick skillet over medium-high heat; add first 4
ingredients. Bring mixture to a boil, and cook 8 minutes, stirring constantly. Reduce heat to medium-low; stir in milk, and cook 1 minute.
Remove from heat, and stir in 1½ teaspoons butter. Set aside, and
keep warm.

2. Rinse and dry skillet. Heat skillet over medium-high heat; add
cumin, salt, pepper, and 1 tablespoon butter, stirring well. Add fish,
and cook 5 minutes on each side or until fish flakes easily when tested
with a fork.

3. Place fish on individual serving plates; spoon sauce evenly over fish.
Garnish with orange slices, if desired. Serve immediately. Yield: 4
servings (serving size: 1 grouper fillet and ¼ cup sauce).

Pan-Seared Mahimahi with Tropical Salsa photo, page 61

POINTS:

3

exchanges:

1 Fruit

3 Very Lean Meat

per serving:

Calories 154

Carbohydrate 13.8g

Fat 1.1g (saturated 0.3g)

Fiber 1.8g

Protein 21.6g

Cholesterol 83mg

Sodium 250mg

Calcium 44mg

Iron 1.7mg

1   cup diced peeled fresh papaya (about ½ medium papaya)
⅔   cup chopped fresh pineapple
1   kiwifruit, peeled and chopped
1   jalapeño pepper, seeded and minced
3   tablespoons finely chopped red onion
2   tablespoons chopped fresh cilantro
2   tablespoons fresh pineapple juice
4   (4-ounce) mahimahi or other firm white fish fillets
¼   teaspoon salt
¼   teaspoon pepper
Cooking spray

1. Combine first 7 ingredients in a medium bowl; toss gently. Cover and chill.

2. Sprinkle fish with salt and pepper. Heat a large nonstick skillet over high heat until hot. Coat fish with cooking spray; add fish to skillet. Cook fish 1 minute on each side or just until lightly browned. Reduce heat to medium, and cook, uncovered, 7 minutes or until fish flakes easily when tested with a fork.

3. Place fish on individual serving plates, and spoon salsa over fish. Yield: 4 servings (serving size: 1 mahimahi fillet and ½ cup salsa).

quick tip: The peppery seeds of the papaya are edible. Reserve about 1 tablespoon to add to the salsa for additional flavor, if desired.

Citrus-Poached Orange Roughy

4   (6-ounce) orange roughy fillets
Cooking spray
½   teaspoon grated orange rind
⅓   cup fresh orange juice
2   tablespoons lime juice
¼   teaspoon salt
¼   teaspoon crushed red pepper flakes
2   tablespoons chopped green onions

POINTS:

3

exchanges:

4 Very Lean Meat

per serving:

Calories 130
Carbohydrate 3.1g
Fat 1.3g (saturated 0.0g)
Fiber 0.2g
Protein 25.2g
Cholesterol 34mg
Sodium 255mg
Calcium 57mg
Iron 0.4mg

1. Arrange fish in a single layer in a 13- x 9-inch baking dish coated with cooking spray.

2. Combine orange rind and next 4 ingredients in a small bowl, stirring well. Pour mixture over fish, and bake at 400° for 20 minutes or until fish flakes easily when tested with a fork.

3. Remove fish from dish with a wide spatula, and place on a serving dish. Sprinkle fish evenly with green onions. Yield: 4 servings (serving size: 1 orange roughy fillet).

meal idea: Serve with angel hair pasta and a mixed greens salad.

Honeyed Salmon over Minted Citrus Salad photo, cover

POINTS:
6

exchanges:
1 Vegetable
1 Fruit
3 Lean Meat

per serving:
Calories 286
Carbohydrate 20.4g
Fat 11.1g (saturated 1.9g)
Fiber 4.4g
Protein 25.8g
Cholesterol 74mg
Sodium 345mg
Calcium 92mg
Iron 2.9mg

2   tablespoons reduced-sodium soy sauce
1½ tablespoons honey
1   tablespoon brown sugar
2   (4-ounce) salmon fillets
1   (26-ounce) jar refrigerated fresh citrus sections in light syrup
2   teaspoons chopped fresh mint
1   teaspoon honey
½   teaspoon vegetable oil
⅛   teaspoon salt
⅛   teaspoon freshly ground pepper
Cooking spray
3   cups packaged trimmed baby spinach

1. Combine soy sauce, 1½ tablespoons honey, and brown sugar in a heavy-duty, zip-top plastic bag. Add fish; seal bag securely, and marinate in refrigerator 1 hour, turning bag occasionally.

2. Drain citrus sections, reserving ¼ cup liquid. Combine citrus with mint; set aside.

3. Combine reserved ¼ cup liquid, 1 teaspoon honey, and vegetable oil; set aside.

4. Remove fish from marinade; discard marinade. Sprinkle fish evenly with salt and pepper.

5. Coat grill rack with cooking spray; place rack over medium-hot coals (350° to 400°). Place fish on rack; grill, covered, 5 minutes on each side or until fish flakes easily when tested with a fork.

6. Arrange spinach evenly on 2 serving plates. Place fish on spinach leaves, and spoon citrus mixture around fish; drizzle evenly with reserved dressing. Yield: 2 servings (serving size: 1 salmon fillet, 1½ cups spinach, ½ cup citrus salad, and about 2 tablespoons dressing).

**Pan-Seared Mahimahi
with Tropical Salsa**
recipe, page 58

Tilapia en Papillote
recipe, page 66

Vegetable Frittata
recipe, page 90

Spinach Pockets
recipe, page 78

prep: 20 minutes   cook: 8 minutes

Snapper with Chunky Romesco Sauce

1   large yellow or red pepper, coarsely chopped
1   small Vidalia or other sweet onion, cut into thin wedges
2   large garlic cloves, minced
Olive oil-flavored cooking spray
4   plum tomatoes, sliced
1   cup chunky garlic and herb tomato sauce (such as Hunt's Ready Sauce)
½   teaspoon salt, divided
¾   teaspoon freshly ground pepper, divided
4   (6-ounce) yellow snapper fillets, skin on
4   teaspoons sliced almonds, toasted

POINTS:

5

exchanges:

3 Vegetable
4½ Very Lean Meat

per serving:

Calories 264
Carbohydrate 15.4g
Fat 5.2g (saturated 0.7g)
Fiber 3.8g
Protein 38.0g
Cholesterol 62mg
Sodium 559mg
Calcium 120mg
Iron 1.8mg

1. Place a large nonstick skillet over medium-high heat until hot. Coat bell pepper, onion, and garlic with cooking spray; add to skillet. Cook, stirring constantly, 5 minutes or until vegetables are tender. Add tomatoes, tomato sauce, ¼ teaspoon salt, and ¼ teaspoon pepper. Bring to a boil; reduce heat, and simmer, covered, 8 minutes. Set aside, and keep warm.

2. Coat fish with cooking spray; sprinkle with remaining ¼ teaspoon salt and remaining ½ teaspoon pepper. Cut three slits in skin side of fish. Place fish in a grill basket coated with cooking spray. Cook, covered, over medium-hot coals (350° to 400°) 4 minutes on each side or until fish flakes easily when tested with a fork.

3. Transfer fish to a serving platter. Spoon sauce over fish; sprinkle with almonds. Yield: 4 servings (serving size: 1 snapper fillet, 1 cup sauce, and 1 teaspoon almonds).

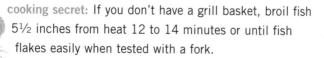

cooking secret: If you don't have a grill basket, broil fish 5½ inches from heat 12 to 14 minutes or until fish flakes easily when tested with a fork.

Tilapia en Papillote photo, page 62

POINTS:

5

exchanges:
1 Vegetable
3 Very Lean Meat
1 Fat

per serving:
Calories 199
Carbohydrate 5.8g
Fat 9.0g (saturated 2.8g)
Fiber 0.8g
Protein 24.1g
Cholesterol 67mg
Sodium 727mg
Calcium 103mg
Iron 0.9mg

2   (4-ounce) tilapia fillets
6   grape tomatoes, halved lengthwise
¼   cup thinly sliced yellow squash (about 1 small)
¼   cup thinly sliced zucchini (about ½ small)
2   tablespoons sliced green onions (about 1 onion)
¼   cup (1 ounce) crumbled feta cheese with garlic and herbs
¼   teaspoon salt
¼   teaspoon freshly ground pepper
3   tablespoons reduced-calorie olive oil vinaigrette (such as Ken's
     Steakhouse)

1. Cut 2 (15- x 13-inch) rectangles of parchment paper; fold each rectangle in half lengthwise. Place parchment sheets on an ungreased baking sheet, and open out flat.

2. Place 1 fillet on half of each parchment sheet near the crease. Place 6 tomato halves, cut side down, on one side of each fillet; place squash and zucchini slices alternately on other side of each fillet. Sprinkle fish with green onions, cheese, salt, and pepper. Drizzle dressing over fish.

3. Fold paper edges over to seal securely; cut off open corners to make a half-moon. Starting with rounded edge of fold, pleat and crimp edges of parchment to make an airtight seal. Bake at 400° for 15 minutes or until packets are puffed.

4. To serve, place packets on individual serving plates. Cut an opening in the top of each packet, and fold paper back. Serve immediately. Yield: 2 servings.

cooking secret: En papillote refers to food baked inside a wrapping of parchment paper.

Grilled Tuna and Mango Salad

3   (5-ounce) tuna fillets
½   teaspoon salt, divided
½   teaspoon freshly ground pepper, divided
Cooking spray
1   cup peeled and cubed mango (about 1 large)
½   cup chopped celery
2   tablespoons chopped pecans, toasted
1½ tablespoons fresh thyme leaves
¼   cup light mayonnaise
2   tablespoons prepared extra-hot horseradish
4   green leaf lettuce leaves

POINTS:

7

exchanges:
½ Fruit
4 Lean Meat

per serving:
Calories 287
Carbohydrate 10.6g
Fat 13.5g (saturated 2.5g)
Fiber 1.5g
Protein 30.6g
Cholesterol 52mg
Sodium 543mg
Calcium 32mg
Iron 1.8mg

1. Sprinkle tuna with ¼ teaspoon salt and ¼ teaspoon pepper. Coat
grill rack with cooking spray; place on grill over medium-hot coals
(350° to 400°). Place tuna on rack; grill, covered, about 5 minutes on
each side or until fish flakes easily when tested with a fork. Remove
from grill; cut tuna into bite-size pieces. Let cool 10 minutes.

2. Combine remaining ¼ teaspoon salt, remaining ¼ teaspoon pepper,
mango, and next 5 ingredients. Add tuna; toss gently. Cover and refrig-
erate 30 minutes or until thoroughly chilled.

3. Place a lettuce leaf on each of 4 individual serving plates. Spoon
about 1 cup tuna mixture onto each lettuce leaf. Yield: 4 servings.

quick tip: This flavorful salad received our highest rating.
Serve it with crusty French bread.

Crawfish Risotto

POINTS:
8

exchanges:
3 Starch
1 Vegetable
3 Very Lean Meat
½ Fat

per serving:
Calories 403
Carbohydrate 50.0g
Fat 6.8g (saturated 3.8g)
Fiber 2.1g
Protein 31.6g
Cholesterol 174mg
Sodium 1248mg
Calcium 183mg
Iron 5.1mg

2   tablespoons light butter
1   small fennel bulb, thinly sliced
1   (8-ounce) package Arborio rice with saffron (such as Alessi)
1   (14½-ounce) can fat-free, reduced-sodium chicken broth
½   cup water
¼   cup dry white wine
1   pound frozen peeled and deveined crawfish tails, thawed,
      rinsed and drained
1   cup frozen green peas, thawed
⅓   cup freshly grated Parmesan cheese

1. Melt butter in a medium saucepan over medium-high heat. Add fennel; cook, stirring constantly, 2 minutes. Add rice; cook, uncovered, 2 minutes, stirring occasionally. Add chicken broth, water, and wine; bring to a boil. Cover, reduce heat, and simmer 10 minutes, stirring occasionally. Add crawfish; simmer, covered, 15 additional minutes or until liquid is absorbed and rice is tender, stirring occasionally. Stir in peas and cheese; let stand 5 minutes. Yield: 4 servings (serving size: 1½ cups).

cooking secret: To prepare fennel, first rinse it thoroughly. Trim the stalks to within 1 inch of the bulb. Discard the hard outside stalks, and reserve the leaves for another use. Cut a slice off the bottom of the bulb. Cut out the tough core from the bottom of the bulb. Starting at one side, cut the bulb lengthwise into ¼-inch-thick slices.

Lobster with Roasted Sweet Corn Rémoulade

Cooking spray

2 cups fresh yellow corn, cut from cob (3 large ears)

8 cups water

3 tablespoons crawfish, shrimp, and crab boil (such as Zatarain's)

2 (8-ounce) fresh or frozen lobster tails, thawed

¼ cup light mayonnaise

2 tablespoons Creole mustard

1½ tablespoons chopped fresh parsley

⅛ teaspoon salt

⅛ teaspoon freshly ground pepper

4 small French rolls (such as Earth Grains)

POINTS:

6

exchanges:

2½ Starch

2 Very Lean Meat

1 Fat

per serving:

Calories 310

Carbohydrate 41.6g

Fat 7.2g (saturated 1.3g)

Fiber 3.6g

Protein 20.5g

Cholesterol 72mg

Sodium 656mg

Calcium 78mg

Iron 1.5mg

1. Coat a jellyroll pan with cooking spray. Spread corn in pan. Broil 3 inches from heat 10 minutes, stirring occasionally. Remove from pan, and spread out to cool. Set aside.

2. Bring water to a boil in a 3-quart saucepan; add crawfish, shrimp, and crab boil. Return to a boil. Reduce heat, and simmer, uncovered, 1 minute. Add lobster tails; return to a boil. Reduce heat, and simmer, uncovered, 5 minutes.

3. Remove lobster tails, and place on a cutting board. Cut down center of lobster tails with heavy scissors; spread opening apart, and remove lobster meat. Coarsely chop lobster. Set aside.

4. Combine mayonnaise and next 4 ingredients in a medium bowl; add reserved lobster and corn, stirring gently. Split rolls to, but not through, bottom of roll; spoon about ½ cup mixture into each roll. Yield: 4 servings (serving size: 1 roll).

Basil Shrimp Kabobs

POINTS:

4

exchanges:

2 Vegetable

1½ Very Lean Meat

1½ Fat

per serving:

Calories 167

Carbohydrate 9.5g

Fat 8.5g (saturated 1.2g)

Fiber 2.1g

Protein 13.3g

Cholesterol 86mg

Sodium 168mg

Calcium 48mg

Iron 2.3mg

¼ cup white wine vinegar

2 tablespoons olive oil

2 teaspoons Dijon mustard

1 garlic clove, cut in half

12 fresh basil leaves

½ pound peeled, deveined large fresh shrimp

1 small red onion, quartered and separated

1 medium green bell pepper, cut into 1-inch pieces

½ (8-ounce) package whole fresh mushrooms

12 cherry tomatoes

Cooking spray

1. Combine first 5 ingredients in container of an electric blender; cover and process until smooth. Transfer to a small bowl.

2. Thread shrimp, onion, pepper, and mushrooms alternately onto 4 (15-inch) skewers; brush with basil sauce. Thread cherry tomatoes onto 2 (15-inch) skewers; brush with basil sauce.

3. Coat a grill rack with cooking spray; place on grill over medium-hot coals (350° to 400°). Place shrimp kabobs on rack; grill, covered, 10 minutes or until shrimp turn pink and vegetables are crisp-tender, turning and basting occasionally with basil sauce. Place tomato kabobs on rack; grill, covered, 3 to 4 minutes, basting occasionally with basil sauce. Serve immediately. Yield: 4 servings (serving size: 1 skewer and 3 tomatoes).

cooking secret: In terms of taste, efficiency, and appearance, there is no difference between metal and wooden skewers. But if you use wooden skewers, remember to soak them in water 10 minutes before using.

Rosemary-Garlic Shrimp with Fettuccine

2   quarts water

8   ounces uncooked fettuccine

1   tablespoon butter or stick margarine

1   teaspoon olive oil

¼   cup all-purpose flour

1¼   pounds large shrimp, peeled

8   garlic cloves, minced

2   tablespoons chopped fresh rosemary

1½   cups dry white wine

2   tablespoons lemon juice

5   plum tomatoes, quartered and peeled, if desired

½   cup chopped green onions (about 6 onions)

1   teaspoon salt

⅛   teaspoon freshly ground pepper

POINTS:

8

exchanges:

3½ Starch

1 Vegetable

3 Very Lean Meat

1 Fat

per serving:

Calories 431

Carbohydrate 58.1g

Fat 7.4g (saturated 2.6g)

Fiber 5.0g

Protein 32.8g

Cholesterol 180mg

Sodium 809mg

Calcium 143mg

Iron 6.9mg

1. Bring water to a rolling boil. Add pasta; cook 12 minutes. Drain; set aside, and keep warm.

2. Heat butter and olive oil in a large nonstick skillet over medium heat. Sprinkle flour over shrimp, tossing to coat well. Add shrimp to skillet; cook, stirring constantly, 4 minutes or until shrimp turn pink and are lightly browned. Remove shrimp from skillet; set aside, and keep warm.

3. Add garlic and rosemary to skillet; cook 1 minute. Add wine, lemon juice, and tomatoes. Increase heat to high, and cook 7 minutes or until most of liquid evaporates. Return shrimp to skillet; cook just until heated. Add green onions, salt, and pepper. Serve over pasta. Yield: 4 servings (serving size: 1 cup shrimp mixture and 1 cup pasta).

Shrimp and Grits Creole

POINTS:

5

exchanges:

2 Starch

1 Vegetable

1½ Very Lean Meat

per serving:

Calories 246

Carbohydrate 34.0g

Fat 2.7g (saturated 0.3g)

Fiber 3.2g

Protein 19.8g

Cholesterol 114mg

Sodium 928mg

Calcium 109mg

Iron 3.8mg

1   cup stone-ground grits
4   cups water
½   cup freshly grated garlic and herb-flavored Parmesan cheese
Olive oil-flavored cooking spray
⅔   cup chopped carrot (about 1 large)
½   cup chopped green bell pepper (about 1 small)
2   (14.5-ounce) cans zesty diced tomatoes with jalapeño peppers
     (such as Del Monte), undrained
½   cup water
2   teaspoons salt-free Cajun seasoning
1¼ pounds large fresh shrimp, peeled and deveined

1. Cook grits according to package directions, using 4 cups water. Stir in Parmesan cheese; set aside, and keep warm.

2. Coat a large saucepan with cooking spray; place over medium-high heat until hot. Add carrot and green pepper; cook 3 minutes, stirring often. Add tomatoes, ½ cup water, and Cajun seasoning. Bring to a boil; cover, reduce heat, and simmer 5 minutes. Add shrimp, and cook 3 minutes or until shrimp turn pink. Spoon ⅔ cup grits into each of 6 individual serving bowls; spoon about ½ cup shrimp mixture over grits. Yield: 6 servings.

cooking secret: Temper the spiciness of this dish by substituting one can of plain diced tomatoes for one can of the zesty type.

Seafood Pot Pie

½   pound peeled, deveined medium fresh shrimp

½   pound bay scallops

½   teaspoon freshly ground pepper

Butter-flavored cooking spray

1   (10¾-ounce) can reduced-fat, reduced-sodium cream of
     mushroom soup

⅔   cup fat-free half-and-half

2   (14-ounce) packages frozen baby gourmet potato blend, thawed
     (such as Birds Eye)

¼   cup coarsely chopped fresh basil

½   teaspoon salt

3   sheets frozen phyllo pastry, thawed

POINTS:

7

exchanges:

2½ Starch

1 Vegetable

3 Very Lean Meat

per serving:

Calories 339

Carbohydrate 42.5g

Fat 4.0g (saturated 1.0g)

Fiber 2.8g

Protein 27.8g

Cholesterol 107mg

Sodium 904mg

Calcium 150mg

Iron 3.0mg

1. Combine first 3 ingredients, tossing well. Place a large nonstick skillet over medium-high heat. Coat shrimp mixture with cooking spray. Add to skillet, and cook 2 minutes, stirring often. Remove from heat.

2. Combine soup and half-and-half in a large bowl, stirring with a whisk. Add shrimp mixture, potato blend, basil, and salt, tossing gently. Pour mixture into a 1½-quart square baking dish coated with cooking spray.

3. Cut phyllo pastry in half crosswise. Work with only one sheet at a time, keeping remaining sheets covered with a damp towel. Coat one side of each sheet with cooking spray, and place lengthwise, coated side up, over shrimp mixture. Repeat procedure with remaining phyllo pastry, alternately placing phyllo crosswise and lengthwise over dish. Fold edges under, and gently press against sides of baking dish.

4. Bake at 375° for 30 to 35 minutes or until golden. Yield: 4 servings.

Lowcountry Boil

POINTS:

7

exchanges:

3½ Starch

4 Very Lean Meat

per serving:

Calories 381

Carbohydrate 49.4g

Fat 4.6g (saturated 1.1g)

Fiber 5.3g

Protein 38.1g

Cholesterol 197mg

Sodium 966mg

Calcium 111mg

Iron 5.6mg

9	cups water
⅓	cup Old Bay seasoning
1	pound small round red potatoes
1	head garlic, separated into cloves and peeled
4	ears fresh yellow corn, halved
½	pound reduced-fat smoked sausage, cut into 2-inch pieces
1	pound unpeeled large fresh shrimp
½	teaspoon salt
½	teaspoon freshly ground pepper
¼	cup chopped fresh parsley

1. Combine first 4 ingredients in a large Dutch oven; bring to a boil. Cook, uncovered, 16 minutes. Add corn and sausage; cook 5 minutes. Add shrimp; cook 3 minutes. Using a slotted spoon, remove vegetables, sausage, and shrimp to a serving platter; discard cooking liquid. Sprinkle vegetables, sausage, and shrimp with salt, pepper, and parsley; toss well. Yield: 4 servings.

quick tip: It takes almost as long to boil the water for this easy entrée as it does to cook it. So, put the water on to boil first thing while you're gathering the ingredients.

Meatless Main Dishes

Pizzettes with Greens

POINTS:

5

exchanges:

2 Starch

1½ Vegetable

½ Lean Meat

1 Fat

per serving:

Calories 265

Carbohydrate 38.4g

Fat 6.5g (saturated 2.5g)

Fiber 3.4g

Protein 13.6g

Cholesterol 10mg

Sodium 707mg

Calcium 220mg

Iron 3.0mg

1   (10-ounce) can refrigerated pizza crust dough

Cooking spray

3   plum tomatoes, thinly sliced

1   tablespoon diced red onion

½   (10-ounce) package frozen asparagus spears, thawed and drained
       (12 spears)

½   cup (2 ounces) freshly grated Parmesan cheese

4   cups gourmet salad greens

2   tablespoons fat-free balsamic vinaigrette

1. Unwrap pizza dough; do not unroll dough. Cut roll of dough into 4 even slices. Place dough, cut side down, on a baking sheet coated with cooking spray. Press dough with fingertips into 5-inch circles. Bake at 425° for 7 minutes. Remove crusts from oven.

2. Top crusts evenly with tomato slices and onion. Top each crust with 3 asparagus spears and 2 tablespoons cheese. Bake at 425° for 10 minutes or until crust is lightly browned and cheese is melted.

3. Combine salad greens and vinaigrette in a medium bowl, and toss gently to coat. To serve, place 1 cup greens on each of 4 serving plates. Place each pizzette next to bed of greens. Yield: 4 servings.

 meal idea: Pick up cubed fresh melon and reduced-fat oatmeal cookies to round out the meal.

Grilled Portobello Pizzas

½   cup finely chopped fresh basil
2   teaspoons olive oil
1   teaspoon bottled minced roasted garlic
12 plum tomatoes, seeded and chopped
1½ tablespoons minced fresh thyme
1   teaspoon olive oil
1   tablespoon bottled minced roasted garlic
4   (4-inch) portobello mushroom caps
Cooking spray
¼   teaspoon salt
¼   teaspoon pepper
½   cup (2 ounces) shredded part-skim mozzarella cheese

POINTS:

5

exchanges:
4 Vegetable
1 Lean Meat
2 Fat

per serving:
Calories 250
Carbohydrate 22.8g
Fat 12.6g (saturated 4.1g)
Fiber 6.7g
Protein 17.6g
Cholesterol 15mg
Sodium 470mg
Calcium 264mg
Iron 3.2mg

1. Combine first 3 ingredients in a small bowl; stir well, and set aside. Combine tomato and next 3 ingredients in a medium bowl; stir well, and set aside.

2. Remove brown gills from the undersides of mushrooms with a spoon; discard gills. Coat top and bottom of mushroom caps evenly with cooking spray; sprinkle with salt and pepper.

3. Coat grill rack with cooking spray; place rack on grill over medium-hot coals (350° to 400°). Place mushrooms, top side up, on rack; grill, covered, 4 minutes. Turn mushrooms over; spoon tomato mixture evenly into caps; top each mushroom with 1 tablespoon basil mixture and 2 tablespoons cheese. Grill, covered, 4 minutes or until mushrooms are tender and cheese melts. Yield: 2 servings (serving size: 2 mushrooms).

Spinach Pockets photo, page 64

POINTS:

7

exchanges:

2½ Starch
2 Vegetable
1 Medium-Fat Meat
1 Fat

per serving:

Calories 365
Carbohydrate 47.4g
Fat 10.5g (saturated 2.7g)
Fiber 5.0g
Protein 20.3g
Cholesterol 13mg
Sodium 1252mg
Calcium 298mg
Iron 5.1mg

¾ cup 2% reduced-fat cottage cheese
2 tablespoons commercial pesto
1 (10-ounce) package frozen chopped spinach, thawed, drained,
    and squeezed dry
¼ teaspoon salt
¼ teaspoon pepper
1 (10-ounce) can refrigerated pizza crust dough
Cooking spray
1 cup sliced fresh mushrooms
½ cup (2 ounces) shredded part-skim mozzarella cheese
1⅓ cups fire-roasted tomato and garlic pasta sauce (such as Classico)

1. Add first 5 ingredients to food processor bowl; pulse 10 times. Set aside.

2. Roll out pizza dough; cut into 4 squares. Place on a baking sheet coated with cooking spray. Roll each square to ⅛-inch thickness. Spoon one-fourth of spinach mixture onto center of each square; top evenly with mushrooms and mozzarella cheese. Moisten edges of each square with water; bring corners to center, pressing edges to seal. Bake at 425° for 12 to 14 minutes or until golden. Serve with pasta sauce. Yield: 4 servings (serving size: 1 pocket and ⅓ cup pasta sauce).

meal idea: Serve these calzone-like pockets with a tossed salad and lemon sorbet.

Macaroni and Cheese with Broccoli

4   ounces elbow macaroni, uncooked (1 cup uncooked pasta)
2   cups fresh broccoli flowerets
1   cup (4 ounces) finely shredded reduced-fat sharp Cheddar cheese
½   cup 1% low-fat cottage cheese
⅓   cup low-fat sour cream
¼   cup fat-free milk
1   large egg, lightly beaten
¼   teaspoon salt
¼   teaspoon pepper

1. Cook macaroni in a Dutch oven according to package directions, omitting salt and fat. Add broccoli during last 2 minutes of cooking time; drain well.

2. Add Cheddar cheese and remaining 6 ingredients to Dutch oven; stir in macaroni mixture. Cook over medium heat, stirring constantly, 6 minutes or until bubbly. Yield: 3 servings (serving size: 1 cup).

quick tip: Broccoli is an easy and healthy addition to this traditional dish. It's one of the best foods you can eat, packed with nutrients such as vitamin C and folate. For the creamiest macaroni and cheese, shred the cheese yourself rather than using preshredded.

POINTS:

8

exchanges:
2 Starch
1 Vegetable
2½ Lean Meat
½ Fat

per serving:
Calories 353
Carbohydrate 36.6g
Fat 11.5g (saturated 7.0g)
Fiber 2.3g
Protein 25.4g
Cholesterol 102mg
Sodium 665mg
Calcium 467mg
Iron 1.2mg

Spinach Spaghetti Bake

POINTS:

7

exchanges:

2 Starch

2½ Vegetable

1 Medium-Fat Meat

1 Fat

per serving:

Calories 337

Carbohydrate 41.6g

Fat 10.4g (saturated 5.0g)

Fiber 4.6g

Protein 18.5g

Cholesterol 61mg

Sodium 919mg

Calcium 388mg

Iron 2.6mg

1   (7-ounce) package spaghetti, uncooked
1   cup preshredded carrot
Cooking spray
1   (26-ounce) jar fire-roasted tomato and garlic pasta sauce (such as
     Classico)
1   cup part-skim ricotta cheese
1   large egg, lightly beaten
¾   teaspoon salt, divided
1   teaspoon olive oil
4   garlic cloves, minced
1   (10-ounce) package trimmed fresh spinach
1   cup (4 ounces) shredded part-skim mozzarella cheese

1. Cook spaghetti in a Dutch oven according to package directions, omitting salt and fat. Add carrot to spaghetti during last 2 minutes of cooking time. Drain. Place pasta mixture in an 11- x 7-inch baking dish coated with cooking spray; stir in pasta sauce. Set aside.

2. Combine ricotta cheese, egg, and ½ teaspoon salt in a small bowl; stir until smooth. Spread ricotta mixture over pasta mixture.

3. Heat olive oil in Dutch oven over medium-high heat until hot; add garlic, spinach, and remaining ¼ teaspoon salt. Cover and cook 2 minutes or until spinach begins to wilt; cook, uncovered, stirring constantly, 3 minutes or until liquid evaporates. Arrange spinach over ricotta mixture. Sprinkle mozzarella cheese over top of spinach.

4. Cover and bake at 350° for 20 minutes. Uncover and bake an additional 5 minutes or until thoroughly heated and mozzarella cheese melts. Yield: 6 servings.

Ravioli with Roasted Red Pepper Sauce

1   teaspoon olive oil
¾   cup chopped onion (about 1 small)
2   garlic cloves, minced
½   cup vegetable broth
2   teaspoons sugar
2   teaspoons red wine vinegar
1   tablespoon plus 1½ teaspoons chopped fresh basil
1   (12-ounce) bottle roasted red bell peppers, drained
½   (25-ounce) package frozen cheese ravioli
¼   cup (1 ounce) finely shredded fresh Parmesan cheese
2   tablespoons thinly sliced fresh basil

POINTS:

7

exchanges:
3 Starch
2 Vegetable
1½ Fat

per serving:
Calories 358
Carbohydrate 52.8g
Fat 10.2g (saturated 5.3g)
Fiber 2.8g
Protein 14.0g
Cholesterol 31mg
Sodium 770mg
Calcium 237mg
Iron 1.3mg

1. Heat oil in a medium nonstick skillet over medium-high heat. Add onion and garlic; cook, stirring constantly, 3 minutes or until tender. Place onion mixture, broth, and next 4 ingredients in a food processor bowl; process until smooth. Return sauce to skillet; cook over medium-high heat 5 minutes or until thoroughly heated.

2. Cook ravioli in a Dutch oven according to package directions, omitting salt and fat. Drain well. Place about 9 ravioli on each of 3 serving plates. Spoon sauce evenly over ravioli. Sprinkle evenly with cheese and sliced fresh basil. Yield: 3 servings.

quick tip: Keep your pantry stocked with jars of roasted red peppers, and you'll have the foundation for a simple sauce when time is short.

Tortellini with Swiss Chard photo, page 3

POINTS:
8

exchanges:
3½ Starch
1½ Vegetable
½ Medium-Fat Meat
1½ Fat

per serving:
Calories 409
Carbohydrate 60.0g
Fat 11.6g (saturated 6.1g)
Fiber 4.6g
Protein 17.2g
Cholesterol 45mg
Sodium 927mg
Calcium 301mg
Iron 5.6mg

2   (9-ounce) containers portobello mushroom tortellini
     (such as DiGiorno)
1   tablespoon extra-virgin olive oil, divided
2   garlic cloves, minced
1¼ pounds Swiss chard, chopped
¼   cup water
½   teaspoon salt
½   teaspoon freshly ground pepper

1. Cook pasta in a Dutch oven according to package directions, omitting salt and fat. Drain; set aside, and keep warm.

2. Heat 2 teaspoons olive oil in a large nonstick skillet over medium heat. Add garlic; cook, stirring constantly, 1 minute or until lightly browned. Add Swiss chard, water, and salt. Cover, reduce heat to medium-low, and cook 10 minutes or until chard is tender. Increase heat to medium-high, and cook, uncovered, 3 minutes or until liquid evaporates, stirring occasionally.

3. Combine chard, tortellini, and pepper in a large serving bowl; toss well. Drizzle with remaining 1 teaspoon olive oil. Yield: 4 servings (serving size: 2 cups).

quick tip: Swiss chard is a member of the beet family and is a good source of vitamins A and C. It has broad green leaves similar to spinach and ribs like celery. The ribs can be white, ruby, or golden. Use both the ribs and leaves in this easy pasta dish.

Tofu-Cheese Stuffed Manicotti

1 (8-ounce) package manicotti shells, uncooked
1¼ cups (5 ounces) shredded part-skim mozzarella cheese, divided
1 (15-ounce) container fat-free ricotta cheese
1 (12.3-ounce) package lite silken firm tofu, drained
¼ cup minced fresh basil or parsley
3 tablespoons grated Parmesan cheese
2 large egg whites, lightly beaten
¼ teaspoon salt
¼ teaspoon pepper
1 (26-ounce) jar pasta sauce with burgundy wine (such as Five
    Brothers)

POINTS:

8

exchanges:

1½ Starch
1½ Lean Meat
2 Skim Milk

per serving:

Calories 378
Carbohydrate 42.8g
Fat 9.2g (saturated 3.4g)
Fiber 4.2g
Protein 31.8g
Cholesterol 15mg
Sodium 840mg
Calcium 677mg
Iron 2.6mg

1. Cook pasta in a Dutch oven according to directions, omitting salt and fat. Drain. Cover and keep warm.

2. Combine ¼ cup mozzarella cheese and next 7 ingredients in a large bowl. Fill cooked manicotti shells evenly with mozzarella cheese mixture.

3. Cover bottom of a 13- x 9-inch baking dish with ⅓ cup pasta sauce. Place stuffed manicotti shells over pasta sauce. Cover with remainder of pasta sauce. Cover and bake at 400° for 30 minutes. Sprinkle with remaining 1 cup cheese. Bake an additional 5 minutes or until cheese melts. Yield: 6 servings (serving size: 2 manicotti).

super food: Tofu is a soy product that lends an extra creamy texture to this dish. Soy's cancer-fighting phytoestrogens, cholesterol-lowering ability, and possible ability to help prevent osteoporosis make it a nutritional powerhouse.

Vegetable Lasagna

POINTS:

8

exchanges:

3½ Starch

3 Vegetable

½ Medium-Fat Meat

1 Fat

per serving:

Calories 426

Carbohydrate 67.5g

Fat 8.1g (saturated 3.9g)

Fiber 6.2g

Protein 21.4g

Cholesterol 23mg

Sodium 665mg

Calcium 378mg

Iron 3.4mg

3   quarts water
10   uncooked lasagna noodles
1½ cups chopped onion
1¼ teaspoons vegetable oil
2   (1-pound) packages frozen broccoli, carrot, and cauliflower mix
1¼ teaspoons salt, divided
¼   teaspoon pepper
½   cup water
½   cup all-purpose flour
2½ cups fat-free milk
1   cup (4 ounces) shredded Gruyère cheese, divided
Cooking spray

1. Bring 3 quarts water to a boil in a Dutch oven. Add lasagna noodles; cook 11 minutes or just until tender. Drain well. Cut in half crosswise, and set aside.

2. Cook onion in hot oil in pan over medium-high heat 5 minutes or until tender. Add vegetable mix, ½ teaspoon salt, pepper, and ½ cup water. Bring to a boil; cover, reduce heat, and simmer 7 minutes or until tender. Uncover; increase heat to high, and cook until liquid evaporates. Set aside.

3. Combine flour, milk, and remaining ¾ teaspoon salt in a medium saucepan; beat with a whisk until smooth. Cook over medium-high heat, whisking constantly, until thickened and bubbly. Cook an additional 2 minutes. Remove from heat, and stir in ¾ cup plus 2 tablespoons Gruyère cheese. Stir 1½ cups cheese sauce into vegetable mixture.

4. Place 5 lasagna noodle halves in bottom of a 9-inch square baking dish coated with cooking spray. Top with one-third of vegetable mixture and 5 lasagna noodles. Repeat process with remaining vegetable mixture and lasagna noodles, ending with lasagna noodles. Pour remaining cheese sauce over top of lasagna noodles and sprinkle with remaining 2 tablespoons Gruyère cheese. Bake, uncovered, at 375° for 20 minutes or until golden. Let stand 15 minutes. Yield: 6 servings.

prep: 15 minutes   cook: 25 minutes   stand: 10 minutes

Enchilada Casserole

Cooking spray

1   (10-ounce) package frozen southwestern style corn and roasted
    red peppers, thawed (such as Green Giant)

1   (19-ounce) can black beans, rinsed and drained

1   teaspoon salt

1   (15-ounce) can red enchilada sauce, divided

13 corn tortillas, cut in half

1½ cups (6 ounces) reduced-fat sharp Cheddar cheese

½   cup chopped fresh cilantro

½   cup fat-free sour cream

POINTS:

6

exchanges:
2½ Starch
1 Medium-Fat Meat
1 Fat

per serving:
Calories 303
Carbohydrate 37.8g
Fat 12.1g (saturated 6.1g)
Fiber 5.5g
Protein 13.4g
Cholesterol 32mg
Sodium 700mg
Calcium 276mg
Iron 1.7mg

1. Coat a medium skillet with cooking spray; place over medium-high heat until hot. Add corn mixture, and cook, stirring constantly, 3 minutes. Add black beans and salt; cook, stirring constantly, 2 minutes. Remove from heat; set aside.

2. Spoon ⅓ cup enchilada sauce over bottom of a 13- x 9-inch baking dish; spread evenly. Arrange 8 tortilla halves over sauce. Spoon half of corn mixture over tortillas; sprinkle with ⅓ cup cheese. Repeat layer with 8 tortilla halves, remaining corn mixture, and ⅓ cup cheese. Top with remaining 10 tortilla halves. Cover with remaining enchilada sauce and remaining cheese.

3. Cover and bake at 400° for 20 minutes. Uncover and bake 5 minutes or until bubbly. Let stand 10 minutes. Sprinkle with cilantro and serve with sour cream. Yield: 8 servings.

meal idea: Serve this southwestern entrée with Pineapple-Mango Salad (page 120).

Vegetable Fried Rice

POINTS:

6

exchanges:

3 Starch
1 Vegetable
1 Lean Meat
½ Fat

per serving:

Calories 336
Carbohydrate 51.1g
Fat 6.8g (saturated 1.1g)
Fiber 8.9g
Protein 16.9g
Cholesterol 1mg
Sodium 902mg
Calcium 49mg
Iron 2.8mg

½   cup fat-free egg substitute
1¼ teaspoons dark sesame oil, divided
1⅓ cups sliced green onions
1½ cups chilled cooked instant brown rice (cooked without salt or fat)
2   tablespoons low-sodium soy sauce
¼   teaspoon pepper
¼   teaspoon ground ginger
1½ cups frozen baby green peas, thawed and drained

1. Cook egg substitute in ¼ teaspoon sesame oil in a large nonstick skillet or wok until set on bottom (do not stir). Turn and cook an additional minute. Cut cooked egg into thin strips, and set aside.

2. Cook green onions in remaining 1 teaspoon sesame oil in skillet 1 minute. Add rice and next 3 ingredients; cook 2 minutes or until thoroughly heated, stirring often. Gently stir in reserved egg strips and green peas. Serve immediately. Yield: 2 servings (serving size: 2 cups).

cooking secret: If you don't have leftover rice, chill cooked rice in the freezer for 10 minutes.

Red Beans And Rice

1⅓ cups long-grain rice, uncooked
2   cups chopped onion (about 1 large)
2½ cups chopped green bell pepper (about 2 medium)
4   garlic cloves, minced
1   tablespoon olive oil
1   to 2 tablespoons Cajun seasoning
½   teaspoon salt
¼   teaspoon pepper
1   (10-ounce) can diced tomatoes and green chiles, undrained
2   (16-ounce) cans red kidney beans, drained and rinsed
1   cup water

POINTS:

8

exchanges:
4½ Starch
2 Vegetable
1 Fat

per serving:
Calories 416
Carbohydrate 78.8g
Fat 4.6g (saturated 0.6g)
Fiber 16.3g
Protein 15.0g
Cholesterol 0mg
Sodium 891mg
Calcium 90mg
Iron 1.8mg

1. Prepare rice according to package directions, omitting salt and fat. Set aside and keep warm.

2. Cook onion, bell pepper, and garlic in hot olive oil in a Dutch oven 5 minutes or until tender. Add Cajun seasoning, salt, and pepper. Cook 3 minutes, stirring constantly. Stir in tomatoes, beans, and water.

2. Cover, reduce heat, and simmer 10 minutes. Uncover and cook an additional 5 minutes. Spoon over rice. Yield: 4 servings (serving size: 1½ cups bean mixture and 1 cup rice).

super food: Meatless dishes get a nutritious boost from beans, which are a good source of soluble fiber and protein.

prep: 6 minutes   cook: 20 minutes

Vegetable Swiss Omelet

POINTS:
3

exchanges:
1 Vegetable
2 Lean Meat

per serving:
Calories 155
Carbohydrate 4.3g
Fat 6.4g (saturated 2.7g)
Fiber 0.9g
Protein 19.6g
Cholesterol 11mg
Sodium 391mg
Calcium 198mg
Iron 2.5mg

Cooking spray
⅓ cup chopped zucchini
¼ cup chopped green onions
¼ cup chopped tomato
2 large egg whites
¾ cup fat-free egg substitute
2 tablespoons water
¼ teaspoon celery seeds
¼ teaspoon pepper
⅛ teaspoon salt
¼ cup (1 ounce) shredded reduced-fat Swiss cheese

1. Coat a 6-inch skillet with cooking spray. Place over medium-high heat until hot. Add zucchini and onions; cook, stirring constantly, until tender. Add tomato, and cook an additional minute. Transfer vegetables to a small bowl; cover, and keep warm. Set aside.

2. In a medium bowl, beat egg whites at high speed of an electric mixer until stiff peaks form. Combine egg substitute and next 4 ingredients in large bowl. Fold egg whites into egg substitute mixture.

3. Wipe skillet dry. Coat skillet with cooking spray; place over medium heat until hot. Spread half of egg mixture in skillet. Cover, reduce heat to low. Cook 5 minutes or until puffy. Turn omelet; cook 3 minutes or until golden. Slide omelet onto a serving plate. Spoon half of vegetables over half of omelet; sprinkle with 2 tablespoons cheese. Fold omelet in half. Repeat procedure with remaining ingredients. Serve immediately. Yield: 2 servings.

prep: 20 minutes   cook: 28 minutes

Sweet Pepper and Basil Frittata

6   large eggs, lightly beaten
½   cup (2 ounces) shredded fontina cheese
¼   cup (1 ounce) freshly shredded Parmesan cheese
¼   cup thinly sliced fresh basil
½   teaspoon salt, divided
½   teaspoon pepper, divided
1   tablespoon olive oil
1   medium yellow onion, thinly sliced
4   garlic cloves, minced
4   medium red bell peppers, thinly sliced (about 4 cups)
1   bay leaf
3   tablespoons balsamic vinegar

POINTS:

4

exchanges:

2 Vegetable
1 High-Fat Meat
1 Fat

per serving:

Calories 191
Carbohydrate 9.2g
Fat 12.2g (saturated 4.8g)
Fiber 1.8g
Protein 11.8g
Cholesterol 226mg
Sodium 338mg
Calcium 138mg
Iron 1.1mg

1. Combine eggs, cheeses, basil, and ¼ teaspoon salt, and ¼ teaspoon pepper in a large bowl; stir well. Set aside.

2. Heat oil in a 12-inch nonstick skillet with ovenproof handle over medium-high heat until hot. Add onion, garlic, and remaining ¼ teaspoon salt and ¼ teaspoon pepper; cook, stirring constantly, until tender. Add bell pepper and bay leaf to skillet, and cook, stirring constantly, 12 to 15 minutes or until very tender. Discard bay leaf. Spread bell peppers evenly in bottom of skillet, and set aside.

3. Reduce heat to medium-low. Stir egg mixture and pour over bell peppers. Cook 3 to 5 minutes or until sides begin to set. Transfer skillet to oven, and bake, uncovered, at 375° for 6 to 8 minutes or until eggs are completely cooked.

4. Loosen frittata with a spatula on sides and underneath. Turn out onto a plate. Brush bottom and sides with balsamic vinegar. Cut into 6 pieces, and serve immediately. Yield: 6 servings.

Vegetable Frittata <small>photo, page 63</small>

POINTS:
5

exchanges:
2 Vegetable
2½ Lean Meat
1 Fat

per serving:
Calories 244
Carbohydrate 12.9g
Fat 12.3g (saturated 7.6g)
Fiber 2.2g
Protein 21.9g
Cholesterol 36mg
Sodium 592mg
Calcium 261mg
Iron 3.3mg

1 (14-ounce) can quartered artichoke hearts, drained
2 plum tomatoes, seeded and finely chopped
2 tablespoons sliced green onions
1 garlic clove, minced
1 tablespoon light stick butter, melted
2 (8-ounce) cartons fat-free egg substitute
¼ teaspoon pepper
⅛ teaspoon hot sauce
Cooking spray
½ cup (2 ounces) freshly grated Parmesan cheese
½ (8-ounce) package ⅓-less-fat cream cheese (Neufchâtel), quartered

1. Press artichoke hearts between layers of paper towels to remove excess moisture. Combine tomato and green onions in a small bowl; set aside.

2. Cook artichoke hearts and garlic in butter in a small nonstick skillet over medium-high heat 2 minutes. Set aside.

3. Combine egg substitute, pepper, and hot sauce in a small bowl. Pour about ½ cup egg substitute mixture into each of 4 individual oven-proof au gratin dishes coated with cooking spray. Sprinkle with Parmesan cheese. Dot each frittata with cream cheese and sprinkle with tomato mixture. Bake on top shelf of oven at 350° for 5 to 7 minutes or until edges begin to set, but center is still soft. Turn oven to broil. Top frittatas evenly with artichoke mixture. Broil 3 inches from heat 3 to 4 minutes or until browned and set. Serve immediately. Yield: 4 servings.

quick tip: Frittatas are Italian omelets that are round, rather than folded like a traditional omelet. Typically, they are cooked on the stove-top and then finished under the broiler in the oven. We simplified the cooking procedure in this recipe by using only the oven.

Leek Pie

6   cups thinly sliced leek (about 6 medium)
1   tablespoon butter, melted
1   cup water
½   teaspoon salt
¼   teaspoon pepper
1   (9-inch) deep-dish frozen piecrust
⅓   cup (1⅓ ounces) shredded Gruyère cheese
2   large eggs
2   large egg whites
1   cup fat-free milk
1   tablespoon cornstarch

POINTS:

6

exchanges:
1 Starch
3 Vegetable
2½ Fat

per serving:
Calories 267
Carbohydrate 29.5g
Fat 12.6g (saturated 5.6g)
Fiber 1.6g
Protein 9.2g
Cholesterol 91mg
Sodium 428mg
Calcium 174mg
Iron 3.1mg

1. Cook leek in butter in a large skillet over medium-high heat 3 minutes, stirring constantly. Add water, salt, and pepper. Cover, reduce heat, and simmer 10 minutes or until leek is tender. Uncover, increase heat to high, and continue cooking, stirring occasionally, 3 minutes or until liquid evaporates.

2. Bake piecrust at 350° for 9 minutes. Sprinkle cheese in bottom of piecrust; spoon leek mixture over cheese.

3. Whisk together eggs, egg whites, milk and cornstarch in a medium bowl; pour over leek mixture. Bake at 350° for 20 to 23 minutes or until set, shielding after 10 minutes, if necessary. Let stand 10 minutes. Yield: 6 servings.

cooking secret: Prepare leeks by first removing the root, the tough outer leaves, and the tops, leaving 2 inches of dark leaves. Wash the leeks thoroughly and slice thinly.

Crustless Spinach Quiche

POINTS:

5

exchanges:

1 Vegetable

2 Medium-Fat Meat

per serving:

Calories 198

Carbohydrate 5.4g

Fat 10.4g (saturated 6.7g)

Fiber 1.5g

Protein 19.6g

Cholesterol 29mg

Sodium 412mg

Calcium 486mg

Iron 1.2mg

3   ounces ⅓-less-fat cream cheese (Neufchâtel), softened
1   cup fat-free milk
1   cup fat-free egg substitute
¼   teaspoon pepper
3   cups (12 ounces) shredded reduced-fat Cheddar cheese
Cooking spray
1   (10-ounce) package frozen chopped spinach, thawed, drained,
      and squeezed dry
1   (10-ounce) package frozen chopped broccoli, thawed, drained,
      and squeezed dry
1   small onion, finely chopped
5   fresh whole mushrooms, sliced
Salsa (optional)

1. Beat cream cheese in a large bowl at medium speed of an electric mixer until creamy. Add milk, egg substitute, and pepper; beat until smooth. Stir in cheese.

2. Coat a large nonstick skillet with cooking spray; place over medium heat until hot. Cook spinach and next 3 ingredients just until tender and liquid evaporates. Cool slightly.

3. Combine egg mixture and spinach mixture, stirring well. Pour into a 10-inch quiche dish coated with cooking spray. Bake, uncovered, at 350° for 45 to 50 minutes or until center is set. Remove from oven and cool on a wire rack 10 minutes.

4. Cut into 8 pieces, and serve with salsa, if desired. Yield: 8 servings.

Meats
&
Poultry

Beefy Baked Beans

POINTS:

4

exchanges:

2½ Starch

1 Lean Meat

per serving:

Calories 226

Carbohydrate 36.4g

Fat 2.0g (saturated 0.7g)

Fiber 2.6g

Protein 16.4g

Cholesterol 24mg

Sodium 695mg

Calcium 58mg

Iron 2.7mg

1   pound ground round

1½ cups chopped onion (about 1 large)

1   cup chopped green bell pepper (about 1 medium)

1   garlic clove, minced

2   (16-ounce) cans navy beans, drained

1   (15¼-ounce) can lima beans, drained

2   (14½-ounce) cans no-salt-added diced tomatoes, undrained

1   cup barbecue sauce

¼   cup firmly packed brown sugar

2   tablespoons salt-free barbecue spice (such as The Spice Hunter)

1. Cook ground round in a large nonstick skillet over medium heat until browned, stirring until it crumbles. Drain and pat dry with paper towels.

2. Combine cooked beef and remaining 9 ingredients in a 4½-quart electric slow cooker. Cover and cook on high heat setting 1 hour. Reduce heat to low setting, and cook 6 to 7 hours. Yield: 10 servings (serving size: 1 cup).

super food: This simple slow-cooker dish is loaded with heart-healthy soluble fiber, thanks to the beans.

Beef Pizza Portobellos

4   medium portobello mushroom caps (about 1 pound)
Cooking spray
2   teaspoons extra-virgin olive oil
¾   pound ground round
1   tablespoon dried basil
⅛   teaspoon fennel seeds
1   (14-ounce) jar pizza sauce
⅔   cup (2⅔ ounces) shredded part-skim mozzarella cheese

POINTS:

6

exchanges:

3 Vegetable
3 Medium-Fat Meat

per serving:

Calories 297
Carbohydrate 16.5g
Fat 13.5g (saturated 5.5g)
Fiber 3.4g
Protein 27.2g
Cholesterol 41mg
Sodium 704mg
Calcium 209mg
Iron 3.6mg

1. Remove gills from undersides of mushrooms with a spoon. Place mushrooms on a baking sheet coated with cooking spray, underside up. Coat mushrooms with cooking spray. Drizzle ½ teaspoon olive oil over each mushroom. Bake, uncovered, at 400° for 8 minutes or until tender. Remove from oven. Set aside, and keep warm.

2. Cook ground round, basil, and fennel in a nonstick skillet over medium heat until beef is browned, stirring until it crumbles. Drain well.

3. Spoon pizza sauce evenly over mushrooms; top evenly with beef mixture and cheese. Broil 2 minutes or until cheese melts. Yield: 4 servings.

quick tip: Reduce your cook time by cooking the ground round while the portobello mushrooms bake.

Gingered Beef Stir-Fry photo, facing page

POINTS:

9

exchanges:

2½ Starch

2 Vegetable

3 Lean Meat

½ Fat

per serving:

Calories 431

Carbohydrate 47.4g

Fat 13.2g (saturated 5.0g)

Fiber 2.8g

Protein 29.2g

Cholesterol 57mg

Sodium 582mg

Calcium 65mg

Iron 6.1mg

¼   cup low-sodium soy sauce
2   tablespoons water
1   tablespoon sugar
1   tablespoon cornstarch
1   pound flank steak
1   teaspoon sesame oil
1   tablespoon peeled, grated fresh ginger
2   garlic cloves, minced
⅔   cup coarsely chopped red bell pepper
½   (8-ounce package) fresh whole mushrooms, quartered
2   cups fresh or frozen Sugar Snap peas
2   teaspoons toasted sesame seeds
3   cups hot cooked Jasmati rice

1. Combine first 4 ingredients in a small bowl, stirring well. Set aside.

2. Cut steak diagonally across grain into thin slices (about ⅛ inch thick).

3. Add oil to preheated wok. Add steak, and stir-fry 6 minutes. Add ginger and garlic, and stir-fry 1 minute. Push steak to one side of wok. Add pepper and mushrooms; stir-fry 2 minutes or until crisp-tender. Add Sugar Snap peas and sesame seeds, and stir-fry 1 minute.

4. Stir soy sauce mixture, and add to wok, stirring constantly, until sauce is thickened and bubbly. Serve over rice. Yield: 4 servings (serving size: ¾ cup rice and 1¼ cups steak mixture).

 meal idea: Serve with Minted Citrus-Jícama Salad (page 121).

**Veal Cutlets with Merlot
Mushrooms and Zucchini**
recipe, page 102

Spicy Lime Chicken with
Spanish-Style Rice
recipe, page 115

Turkey Sausage, Fennel, and Leek Pizza
recipe, page 117

Slow-Cooker Shredded Beef with Chipotle Peppers

1½ pounds top sirloin steak

Cooking spray

1   (16-ounce) package frozen pepper stir-fry

1   (8-ounce) can tomato sauce

¼   cup steak sauce

½   cup chipotle salsa

1   tablespoon sugar

¼   teaspoon salt

POINTS:

6

exchanges:

2 Vegetable

3 Lean Meat

per serving:

Calories 272

Carbohydrate 11.5g

Fat 9.0g (saturated 3.4g)

Fiber 1.8g

Protein 35.0g

Cholesterol 101mg

Sodium 647mg

Calcium 20mg

Iron 4.2mg

1. Trim fat from steak. Place steak in a 4½-quart electric slow cooker coated with cooking spray. Top with pepper stir-fry. Combine tomato sauce and steak sauce; pour over peppers. Cover and cook on high heat setting 1 hour. Reduce heat to low setting, and cook 7 hours.

2. Remove steak from slow cooker with a slotted spoon. Shred steak with 2 forks. Return shredded steak to slow cooker; turn off slow cooker. Add salsa, sugar, and salt. Cover and let stand 15 minutes. Yield: 6 servings (serving size: about ¾ cup).

meal idea: Serve this saucy dish with mashed potatoes or rice and a simple tossed salad.

Veal Cutlets with Merlot Mushrooms and Zucchini photo, page 98

POINTS:

5

exchanges:

1 Vegetable

4 Lean Meat

per serving:

Calories 242

Carbohydrate 6.7g

Fat 10.2g (saturated 4.6g)

Fiber 1.5g

Protein 31.0g

Cholesterol 115mg

Sodium 608mg

Calcium 234mg

Iron 2.3mg

3   small zucchini, halved lengthwise and sliced

Cooking spray

¾   teaspoon salt, divided

½   teaspoon pepper, divided

2   garlic cloves, minced

1   (8-ounce) package sliced fresh mushrooms

2   tablespoons Merlot or other dry red wine

½   cup sliced green onions

1   pound veal cutlets (¼ inch thick)

½   cup water

⅓   cup (1⅓ ounces) grated Gruyère cheese

1. Place a large nonstick skillet over medium-high heat. Coat zucchini with cooking spray, and sprinkle with ¼ teaspoon salt and ¼ teaspoon pepper. Add zucchini and garlic to skillet; cook, stirring constantly, 3 minutes or until tender. Set aside, and keep warm.

2. Wipe skillet clean with paper towels. Coat mushrooms with cooking spray. Place skillet over medium-high heat until hot. Add mushrooms; cook, stirring constantly, 3 minutes or until golden. Stir in wine, green onions, and ¼ teaspoon salt; cook 2 to 3 minutes or until liquid is absorbed. Set aside, and keep warm.

3. Wipe skillet clean with paper towels. Sprinkle veal evenly with remaining ¼ teaspoon salt and remaining ¼ teaspoon pepper. Coat veal with cooking spray. Place skillet over high heat. Add half of veal, and cook 1 minute on each side or until browned. Repeat procedure with remaining veal. Remove veal from skillet. Set aside; keep warm.

4. Add water to skillet; cook until liquid is reduced to ¼ cup, scraping pan to loosen browned bits. Return mushrooms and veal to skillet; toss to coat with sauce. Sprinkle with cheese, and serve with zucchini. Yield: 4 servings.

Lamb Curry

1	pound lean boned leg of lamb
	Cooking spray
3	cups Vidalia or other sweet onion (about 1 large)
1	(2-inch) piece fresh ginger
1	(14½-ounce) can fat-free beef broth
1	tablespoon curry powder
½	teaspoon salt
6	small red potatoes, quartered (about 1 pound)
2	cups frozen green peas

POINTS:

7

exchanges:

2 Starch

2 Vegetable

3 Lean Meat

per serving:

Calories 344

Carbohydrate 40.4g

Fat 6.4g (saturated 2.2g)

Fiber 7.8g

Protein 32.0g

Cholesterol 73mg

Sodium 815mg

Calcium 69mg

Iron 5.6mg

1. Trim fat from lamb; cut lamb into 1½-inch pieces.

2. Coat lamb with cooking spray. Cook lamb in a large nonstick skillet over medium-high heat 4 to 5 minutes or until browned, stirring occasionally. Remove lamb from skillet; set aside.

3. Add onion and ginger to food processor bowl; process until minced.

4. Coat onion mixture with cooking spray. Cook in skillet over medium-high heat 3 minutes or until lightly browned. Add lamb, broth, curry powder, and salt. Bring to a boil; cover, reduce heat, and simmer 30 minutes, stirring occasionally. Add potato; cover and cook 20 minutes. Add peas; cook 3 additional minutes. Yield: 4 servings (serving size: 1¾ cups).

 quick tip: Vidalia onions have a higher natural sugar and water content than other onion varieties. Store them in a cool, dry place and separate from each other.

Lamb Chops with Caramelized Onions and Swiss Chard

POINTS:

9

exchanges:

1½ Starch

4 Vegetable

4 Lean Meat

1 Fat

per serving:

Calories 406

Carbohydrate 29.0g

Fat 16.7g (saturated 4.6g)

Fiber 6.4g

Protein 39.1g

Cholesterol 108mg

Sodium 548mg

Calcium 161mg

Iron 6.8mg

8   (4-ounce) French-cut lean lamb rib chops

¼   cup reduced-calorie olive oil vinaigrette (such as Ken's Steakhouse)

2   teaspoons olive oil

2   large Vidalia onions, sliced (about 1½ pounds)

2   tablespoons brown sugar

1   tablespoon balsamic vinegar

3   tablespoons water

2   bunches Swiss chard leaves, torn into large pieces (about 1½ pounds)

Cooking spray

1. Trim fat from lamb.

2. Place lamb in a large heavy-duty, zip-top plastic bag; pour vinaigrette over chops. Seal bag, and marinate in refrigerator 8 hours, turning bag occasionally.

3. Pour oil into a large nonstick skillet; place skillet over medium heat until hot. Add onion; cover and cook 20 minutes or until golden, stirring often. Add brown sugar and balsamic vinegar; cook 2 minutes, stirring constantly. Add water; bring to a boil, scraping browned bits. Add Swiss chard; cover and cook 3 minutes or just until wilted, stirring once. Set aside, cover, and keep warm.

4. Coat grill rack with cooking spray; place on grill over medium-hot coals (350° to 400°). Remove lamb from bag, reserving marinade. Place lamb on rack; grill, uncovered, 3 to 5 minutes on each side or until desired degree of doneness, turning occasionally and basting with reserved marinade. Serve with onion mixture. Yield: 4 servings (serving size: 2 chops and ¼ cup onion mixture).

Bourbon Pork Tenderloin with Peach Chutney photo, page 4

1   (1-pound) pork tenderloin
½   cup bourbon
2   tablespoons coarse-ground mustard
1   tablespoon chopped fresh thyme leaves
Cooking spray
2   cups coarsely chopped peeled fresh or frozen peaches, thawed
¼   cup hot mango chutney
1   tablespoon sliced green onions

1. Trim fat from pork. Combine bourbon, mustard, and thyme in a large heavy-duty, zip-top plastic bag. Add tenderloin; marinate in refrigerator 8 hours.

2. Coat grill rack with cooking spray; place on grill over medium-hot coals (350° to 400°). Remove tenderloin from bag, reserving marinade. Place tenderloin on rack. Grill, covered, 9 minutes; turn tenderloin, and brush with marinade. Cover and grill 7 to 9 additional minutes or until meat thermometer inserted into thickest part of tenderloin registers 160°.

3. Combine peaches, chutney, and green onion in a medium bowl, stirring well. Cut pork into thin slices, and spoon peach chutney over slices. Yield: 4 servings.

cooking secret: All bourbon is whiskey, but not all whiskey is bourbon. Bourbon is made from corn and lends a slightly sweet taste to this pork entrée. Another type of whiskey, such as Scotch, won't impart the same flavor. If you don't have bourbon on hand, use this simple substitution: Combine 1 teaspoon vanilla extract and ½ cup apple juice. Proceed with the recipe as directed.

POINTS:
5

exchanges:
½ Starch
1 Fruit
3 Lean Meat

per serving:
Calories 250
Carbohydrate 24.6g
Fat 4.7g (saturated 1.4g)
Fiber 1.8g
Protein 25.2g
Cholesterol 79mg
Sodium 453mg
Calcium 18mg
Iron 1.6mg

Caribbean Pork with Mango Salsa

POINTS:

6

exchanges:

1½ Fruit

3 Lean Meat

per serving:

Calories 271

Carbohydrate 21.0g

Fat 11.7g (saturated 3.9g)

Fiber 5.2g

Protein 22.3g

Cholesterol 57mg

Sodium 347mg

Calcium 36mg

Iron 2.9mg

1   fresh mango, peeled and diced
½   cup finely chopped poblano chile pepper
2   tablespoons frozen orange juice concentrate, thawed
2   tablespoons chopped fresh cilantro
1   tablespoon grated fresh ginger
½   teaspoon sugar
½   teaspoon ground allspice
½   teaspoon pepper
½   teaspoon salt
4   (4-ounce) boneless center-cut pork loin chops (½ inch thick)
Cooking spray

1. Combine first 6 ingredients in a medium bowl, and toss well. Cover and chill.

2. Combine allspice, pepper, and salt in a small bowl; mix well. Sprinkle evenly on one side of pork. Place a large nonstick skillet over medium-high heat until hot. Lightly coat pork with cooking spray. Cook pork, seasoned side down, 6 minutes or until lightly browned. Turn pork, and cook 6 to 7 additional minutes or until done. Serve with mango salsa. Yield: 4 servings (serving size: 1 pork chop and about ⅓ cup mango salsa).

meal idea: Serve this tropical pork dish with yellow rice and blue corn tortilla chips.

Pork Chops with Cranberry Salsa

2   medium-size oranges
1½ cups fresh or frozen cranberries
⅓   cup coarsely chopped green onions
¼   cup fresh mint leaves
¼   cup honey
4   (4-ounce) boneless center-cut pork loin chops (½ inch thick)
½   teaspoon salt
¼   teaspoon pepper
Cooking spray
¼   cup low-sugar orange marmalade

POINTS:
5

exchanges:
1 Starch
1 Fruit
3 Lean Meat

per serving:
Calories 256
Carbohydrate 28.0g
Fat 7.2g (saturated 2.6g)
Fiber 2.9g
Protein 21.2g
Cholesterol 56mg
Sodium 342mg
Calcium 42mg
Iron 1.0mg

1. Grate 2 tablespoons rind from one orange; set grated rind aside.

2. Peel and section oranges over food processor bowl to catch juices. Add orange rind, orange sections, cranberries, and next 3 ingredients; process until coarsely chopped, scraping down sides, if necessary. Cover and chill.

3. Sprinkle pork with salt and pepper; coat with cooking spray. Place a large nonstick skillet over medium-high heat until hot. Add pork; cook 4 minutes on each side. Add marmalade; cook an additional 2 minutes or until pork is done. Place pork on a serving plate; serve with cranberry salsa, using a slotted spoon. Yield: 4 servings (serving size: 1 pork chop and about ½ cup cranberry salsa).

quick tip: If you don't have a food processor, the salsa ingredients can be quickly chopped by hand.

Penne with Prosciutto, Tomatoes, and Rosemary

POINTS:

7

exchanges:

3 Starch

3 Vegetable

½ Medium-Fat Meat

½ Fat

per serving:

Calories 366

Carbohydrate 58.8g

Fat 7.1g (saturated 2.7g)

Fiber 5.4g

Protein 17.4g

Cholesterol 22mg

Sodium 725mg

Calcium 109mg

Iron 3.4mg

1   (8-ounce) package penne pasta, uncooked
¼   pound prosciutto, thinly sliced
1   large onion, halved and sliced
4   large tomatoes, chopped
1½ tablespoons finely chopped fresh rosemary
½   teaspoon salt
½   teaspoon pepper
¼   cup (1 ounce) finely shredded Asiago cheese

1. Cook pasta in a Dutch oven according to package directions, omitting salt and fat. Drain; set aside, and keep warm.

2. Cook prosciutto in a large nonstick skillet over medium-high heat 4 minutes, stirring constantly. Reduce heat to medium, add onion; cook, stirring constantly, 5 minutes or until golden. Increase heat to high, and add tomatoes; cook, stirring constantly, 4 minutes. Stir in rosemary, salt, and pepper; remove from heat, and transfer to a large serving bowl. Add pasta; toss well. Sprinkle with Asiago cheese. Yield: 4 servings (serving size: 1½ cups).

cooking secret: Prosciutto is the Italian word for ham. The ham is seasoned, salt-cured, and air-dried for at least one year. Look for this slightly sweet, paper-thin delicacy in gourmet stores or the deli section of your supermarket. If you're not able to find prosciutto, simply substitute lean ham.

Chicken and Spinach Soft Tacos

Cooking spray

1¼ cups chopped onion

2   garlic cloves, minced

1   (10-ounce) package trimmed fresh spinach, torn

1   (9-ounce) package frozen cooked diced chicken breast, thawed

1   (1.25-ounce) envelope 40%-less-sodium taco seasoning mix

1   cup water

5   (6-inch) corn tortillas

⅓   cup (1⅓ ounces) shredded Monterey Jack cheese with jalapeño
      peppers

⅓   cup chopped tomato

⅓   cup low-fat sour cream

1   tablespoon plus 2 teaspoons chopped green onions

POINTS:

4

exchanges:

1½ Starch

1 Vegetable

1½ Lean Meat

per serving:

Calories 201

Carbohydrate 26.6g

Fat 4.6g (saturated 2.6g)

Fiber 2.4g

Protein 16.0g

Cholesterol 40mg

Sodium 665mg

Calcium 189mg

Iron 2.7mg

1. Coat a large nonstick skillet with cooking spray; place over medium-high heat until hot. Add onion; cook 5 minutes or until lightly browned. Add garlic; cook 30 seconds, stirring constantly.

2. Add spinach and next 3 ingredients; cook, uncovered, 20 minutes or until spinach wilts and most of the liquid is absorbed.

3. Heat tortillas according to package directions. Place about ½ cup chicken mixture on each tortilla. Top each with 1 tablespoon each of cheese, tomato and sour cream, and 1 teaspoon green onions. Yield: 5 servings.

Santa Fe Chicken Enchiladas

POINTS:

4

exchanges:

2 Starch

½ Vegetable

1 Lean Meat

per serving:

Calories 239

Carbohydrate 32.3g

Fat 4.5g (saturated 1.9g)

Fiber 7.3g

Protein 15.6g

Cholesterol 31mg

Sodium 460mg

Calcium 221mg

Iron 2.5mg

1   cup frozen cooked diced chicken breast, thawed
3   tablespoons chopped fresh cilantro, divided
¼   teaspoon pepper
1   (15-ounce) can chunky chili-style tomato sauce (such as Hunt's Ready Sauce)
2   tablespoons water
4   (6-inch) corn tortillas
1   (15-ounce) can black beans, rinsed, drained, and divided
⅓   cup (1⅓ ounces) shredded Monterey Jack cheese, divided
Cooking spray
¼   cup fat-free sour cream

1. Combine chicken, 2 tablespoons cilantro, and pepper in a small bowl; stir well.

2. Combine tomato sauce and water; pour into a plate. Set aside.

3. Microwave 2 tortillas, uncovered, at HIGH 10 seconds; dip each tortilla in sauce mixture. Spoon ¼ cup chicken mixture down center of each tortilla; top each with 2 tablespoons black beans and 1 table-spoon cheese. Roll up tortillas, and place seam sides down in an 8-inch square baking dish coated with cooking spray. Repeat proce-dure with remaining 2 tortillas, sauce mixture, chicken mixture, black beans, and cheese.

4. Pour any remaining tomato sauce mixture over enchiladas; top with remaining black beans and remaining cheese. Bake, uncovered, at 375° for 20 minutes or just until bubbly. Sprinkle with remaining 1 tablespoon cilantro. Serve with sour cream. Yield: 4 servings (serving size: 1 enchilada and 1 tablespoon sour cream).

Homestyle Chicken Pot Pie

Cooking spray

1   pound skinned, boned chicken breast halves, cut into cubes

1   (10¾-ounce) can reduced-fat, reduced-sodium cream of
     chicken soup

½   cup low-fat buttermilk

1   (10-ounce) package frozen mixed vegetables, thawed

1   (8-ounce) baking potato, peeled and diced

1   (2-ounce) jar diced pimiento, drained

½   teaspoon salt

¼   teaspoon pepper

½   (15-ounce) package refrigerated piecrusts

POINTS:

7

exchanges:

1½ Starch

2 Vegetable

2 Very Lean Meat

2 Fat

per serving:

Calories 348

Carbohydrate 34.6g

Fat 12.7g (saturated 3.4g)

Fiber 3.1g

Protein 23.3g

Cholesterol 49mg

Sodium 650mg

Calcium 48mg

Iron 2.1mg

1. Place a large nonstick skillet over medium-high heat until hot. Coat skillet with cooking spray; add chicken, and cook 2 minutes, stirring often. Add soup and buttermilk, stirring well. Bring to a boil over medium-high heat; stir in mixed vegetables and potato. Cover, reduce heat, and simmer 20 minutes or until potato is tender. Stir in pimiento, salt, and pepper; remove from heat.

2. Place piecrust on a baking sheet coated with cooking spray. Bake at 400° for 8 minutes or until lightly browned.

3. Gently slide baked piecrust over mixture in skillet. Yield: 6 servings.

cooking secret: It's easier to cube raw chicken if you freeze it just until it's firm.

Sherried Chicken and Artichokes

POINTS:

4

exchanges:

2½ Vegetable
3 Very Lean Meat

per serving:

Calories 205
Carbohydrate 13.0g
Fat 1.6g (saturated 0.4g)
Fiber 2.8g
Protein 30.8g
Cholesterol 66mg
Sodium 773mg
Calcium 16.2mg
Iron 1.5mg

4   (4-ounce) skinned, boned chicken breast halves
1   tablespoon plus 1½ teaspoons salt-free Greek seasoning, divided
    Cooking spray
1   (8-ounce) package sliced fresh mushrooms
1   (14-ounce) can quartered artichoke hearts, drained
1⅓ cups fat-free, reduced-sodium chicken broth, divided
⅓   cup dry sherry
⅛   teaspoon salt
2½ tablespoons all-purpose flour

1. Place a large nonstick skillet over medium-high heat until hot. Sprinkle chicken on both sides with 1 tablespoon Greek seasoning; coat with cooking spray. Add chicken to skillet; cook 2 minutes on each side or until browned. Transfer chicken to a 2-quart baking dish; set aside.

2. Coat mushrooms and artichoke hearts with cooking spray; add to skillet. Cook, stirring constantly, 2 minutes or until mushrooms are tender; stir into chicken in baking dish.

3. Combine 1 cup chicken broth, sherry, salt, and remaining 1½ teaspoons Greek seasoning in skillet; bring to a boil. Combine remaining ⅓ cup broth and flour, stirring with a whisk until smooth. Stir flour mixture into sherry mixture. Cook 1 minute or until thickened; pour over chicken mixture.

4. Cover and bake at 375° for 35 minutes. Yield: 4 servings.

Braised Chicken Thighs with Lemon and Carrots

½   cup chopped fresh parsley
1   tablespoon grated lemon rind
2   teaspoons olive oil
1½ pounds skinned, boned chicken thighs
1¼ pounds carrots, scraped and diagonally sliced
1   medium onion, halved and sliced
1   teaspoon ground cumin
¾   teaspoon salt
¼   teaspoon pepper
¼   cup fresh lemon juice
½   cup water

POINTS:

4

exchanges:

2 Vegetable
3 Lean Meat

per serving:

Calories 196
Carbohydrate 11.3g
Fat 6.2g (saturated 1.4g)
Fiber 3.2g
Protein 23.6g
Cholesterol 94mg
Sodium 423mg
Calcium 50mg
Iron 2.1mg

1. Combine parsley and lemon rind in a small bowl; set aside.

2. Heat oil in a large nonstick skillet over medium-high heat until hot. Add chicken thighs and cook 6 minutes on each side or until lightly browned. Remove thighs; set aside. Add carrot and onion; cook, stirring constantly, 8 minutes or until tender.

3. Add cumin and remaining 4 ingredients. Return chicken thighs to skillet. Cover, reduce heat, and simmer 15 minutes or until chicken is done. Uncover and increase heat to high. Cook 2 minutes or until liquid thickens. Stir in parsley and lemon rind just before serving. Yield: 6 servings.

super food: Carrots owe their vibrant orange color to the cancer-fighting nutrient beta-carotene. They also contain plenty of natural sugars.

Slow-Cooker Chinese Chicken Soup

POINTS:

3

exchanges:

1 Fruit

2½ Vegetable

1½ Very Lean Meat

per serving:

Calories 185

Carbohydrate 29.9g

Fat 1.8g (saturated 0.4g)

Fiber 5.8g

Protein 14.7g

Cholesterol 39mg

Sodium 1037mg

Calcium 25mg

Iron 1.1mg

1   (15¼-ounce) can pineapple tidbits in juice, undrained

1   (8-ounce) can sliced water chestnuts, undrained

⅓   cup low-sodium soy sauce

¾   to 1 teaspoon Chinese five-spice powder

3   medium carrots, scraped and sliced

4   green onions, diagonally cut into 2-inch pieces

½   teaspoon salt

½   teaspoon pepper

2   (6-ounce) skinned, bone-in chicken breast halves

2   (4-ounce) skinned, bone-in chicken thighs

1. Drain pineapple and water chestnuts, reserving liquids. Add soy sauce and five-spice powder to liquids; stir well.

2. Place pineapple, water chestnuts, carrot, and green onions in a 3½-quart slow cooker. Sprinkle salt and pepper over chicken; place chicken over vegetables. Pour liquid mixture over chicken. Cover and cook on high heat setting 1 hour; reduce heat to low setting, and cook 6 hours.

3. Remove chicken from bones, and shred meat. Add meat to vegetable mixture. Yield: 4 servings (serving size: 1½ cups).

quick tip: Water chestnuts are the health-conscious cook's friend, as they add texture to recipes without excess calories or fat. Serve this Asian-inspired soup with whole wheat rolls and orange sherbet.

Spicy Lime Chicken with Spanish-Style Rice photo, page 99

4   (6-ounce) skinned, bone-in chicken breast halves
⅓   cup fresh lime juice
½   teaspoon ground cumin
½   teaspoon chili powder
⅛   teaspoon ground red pepper
Cooking Spray
Spanish-Style Rice

POINTS:

7

exchanges:

3 Starch
½ Vegetable
3½ Very Lean Meat

per serving:

Calories 358
Carbohydrate 46.7g
Fat 4.2g (saturated 0.3g)
Fiber 6.4g
Protein 33.6g
Cholesterol 74mg
Sodium 1464mg
Calcium 81mg
Iron 3.7mg

1. Place chicken in a heavy-duty, zip-top plastic bag; pour lime juice over chicken. Seal bag, and shake until chicken is well coated. Marinate in refrigerator 1 hour, turning bag occasionally.

2. Combine cumin, chili powder, and red pepper in a small bowl. Remove chicken from marinade, discarding marinade. Sprinkle chicken with cumin mixture.

3. Coat rack of broiler pan with cooking spray. Place chicken, skinned side down, on rack; broil 8 inches from heat 25 minutes. Turn chicken, and broil 15 additional minutes or until done. Serve with Spanish-Style Rice. Yield: 4 servings (serving size: 1 chicken breast and 1 cup rice).

Spanish-Style Rice

2½ cups water
1   (4.5-ounce) can chopped green chiles, undrained
¾   cup chunky salsa
1   (8-ounce) package black beans and rice mix (such as Vigo)
¼   cup minced fresh cilantro

1. Combine first 3 ingredients in a medium saucepan; bring to a boil. Add black beans and rice mix, stir well. Cover and simmer 20 to 25 minutes or until liquid is almost absorbed. Stir in cilantro. Yield: 4 servings.

Duck Breast with Cherry Sauce

POINTS:

6

exchanges:

1 Starch

1 Fruit

3 Lean Meat

per serving:

Calories 272

Carbohydrate 28.0g

Fat 7.3g (saturated 1.8g)

Fiber 1.8g

Protein 24.1g

Cholesterol 87mg

Sodium 443mg

Calcium 24mg

Iron 5.9mg

1   (16-ounce) can pitted dark, sweet cherries in heavy syrup

4   skinned, boned duck breast halves

½   teaspoon salt, divided

1¼ teaspoons Chinese five-spice powder, divided

2   teaspoons olive oil

½   cup finely chopped shallots

½   cup port wine, divided

½   cup fat-free, reduced-sodium chicken broth

1. Drain cherries, reserving ¼ cup of syrup. Set aside.

2. Place duck between 2 sheets of heavy-duty plastic wrap; flatten to even thickness, using a meat mallet or rolling pin. Sprinkle ¼ teaspoon salt and ½ teaspoon Chinese five-spice powder over duck breasts. Heat oil in a large nonstick skillet over medium heat. Add duck; cook 7 minutes on each side or until done. Remove duck from skillet. Set aside, and keep warm.

3. Add shallots to pan and cook, stirring constantly, 1 minute. Add ¼ cup port wine to skillet, stirring to loosen browned bits. Simmer 1 minute. Add remaining ¼ cup port wine, ¼ cup reserved cherry syrup, chicken broth, remaining five-spice powder, and remaining ¼ teaspoon salt; simmer 10 minutes. Add cherries, and simmer 2 minutes. Add duck, and simmer 1 minute. Yield: 4 servings (serving size: 1 duck breast half and ½ cup cherry sauce).

meal idea: Serve with herbed rice pilaf and steamed green beans.

prep: 25 minutes   cook: 10 minutes

Turkey Sausage, Fennel, and Leek Pizza

photo, page 100

½   pound sweet or hot Italian turkey sausage (about 2 links)
1¾ cups very thinly sliced fennel bulb (about 1 large bulb)
1½ cups thinly sliced lengthwise leeks (about 2 medium leeks)
2   teaspoons olive oil
1   (16-ounce) Italian bread shell (such as Boboli)
½   cup pizza sauce
¼   cup thinly sliced red onion
½   cup (2 ounces) shredded part-skim mozzarella cheese
Chopped fennel leaves (optional)

POINTS:

7

exchanges:
2 Starch
2 Vegetable
1 Medium-Fat Meat
1 Fat

per serving:
Calories 330
Carbohydrate 40.3g
Fat 10.9g (saturated 3.5g)
Fiber 2.2g
Protein 18.3g
Cholesterol 36mg
Sodium 792mg
Calcium 318mg
Iron 3.9mg

1. Remove casings from sausage. Cook sausage in a large nonstick skillet over medium-high heat until sausage is browned, stirring until it crumbles. Remove from skillet; set aside.

2. Wipe skillet clean with paper towels. Cook fennel and leek in hot oil, stirring constantly in skillet over medium heat 8 minutes or until vegetables are lightly browned.

3. Place bread shell on an ungreased baking sheet or pizza pan. Spread pizza sauce evenly over crust. Top with cooked vegetables, sausage, onion slices, and cheese.

4. Bake at 450° for 10 minutes or until bubbly. Sprinkle with chopped fennel leaves, if desired. Yield: 6 servings.

quick tip: Fennel tastes a bit like licorice. Leeks are related to garlic and onion. Both fennel and leek lend flavor to dishes without adding excess calories.

Glazed Turkey Cutlets

POINTS:

6

exchanges:

1½ Starch
1 Vegetable
3 Very Lean Meat

per serving:
Calories 291
Carbohydrate 31.2g
Fat 4.6g (saturated 1.0g)
Fiber 1.4g
Protein 29.5g
Cholesterol 68mg
Sodium 227mg
Calcium 32mg
Iron 3.0mg

1⅓ cups uncooked long-grain rice
¼   cup fat-free, reduced-sodium chicken broth
3   tablespoons balsamic vinegar
2   teaspoons honey
¼   teaspoon salt
¼   teaspoon pepper
1   pound turkey breast cutlets (¼-inch-thick)
2   teaspoons olive oil
2   garlic cloves, minced
1   red bell pepper, cut into strips
1   green bell pepper, cut into strips

1. Cook rice in a Dutch oven according to package directions, omitting salt and fat.

2. Combine chicken broth, balsamic vinegar, and honey in a small bowl. Set aside.

3. Sprinkle salt and pepper over both sides of turkey. Heat oil in a large nonstick skillet over medium-high heat until hot. Add garlic; cook, stirring constantly, 30 seconds. Add turkey; cook 2 minutes on each side or until done. Remove from skillet; transfer to a large serving platter, and keep warm. Reduce heat to medium; add bell peppers, and cook, stirring constantly, 2 minutes. Add broth mixture to skillet; cook 30 seconds, stirring constantly. Spoon sauce and peppers over cutlets. Serve with rice. Yield: 4 servings.

quick tip: Keep cook time to a minimum by putting the rice on to cook while you mince the garlic and cut the bell peppers into strips.

Salads

Pineapple-Mango Salad photo, page 136

POINTS:
1

exchanges:
1½ Fruit

per serving:
Calories 77
Carbohydrate 19.2g
Fat 0.2g (saturated 0.1g)
Fiber 2.0g
Protein 0.6g
Cholesterol 0mg
Sodium 2mg
Calcium 17mg
Iron 0.5mg

¾ cup cubed fresh mango (about 1 medium)
1   cup fresh pineapple chunks
¾ cup chopped red bell pepper (about 1 medium)
1   medium orange
2   tablespoons finely chopped jalapeño pepper (about 1 pepper)
1½ tablespoons sugar

1. Combine mango, pineapple, and red bell pepper in a medium bowl; set aside.

2. Grate 1 teaspoon rind from orange; set aside. Peel orange, and cut out sections over a small bowl; squeeze membranes to extract juice. Reserve 2 tablespoons juice. Discard remaining juice and membranes. Add reserved orange rind and sections to mango mixture. Add jalapeño pepper, reserved orange juice, and sugar; toss gently. Let stand 10 minutes. Yield: 5 servings (serving size: about ½ cup).

 super food: Both pineapple and mango are good sources of vitamin C, a powerful nutrient that protects the body from harmful free radicals.

Minted Citrus-Jícama Salad

1   medium jícama, peeled and cut into ¼-inch strips (2 cups)
1   (26-ounce) jar refrigerated fresh citrus sections in light syrup,
        drained
1½ tablespoons sugar
3   tablespoons lime juice
2½ tablespoons chopped fresh mint

POINTS:

2

exchanges:

1 Vegetable

1½ Fruit

per serving:

Calories 107

Carbohydrate 26.6g

Fat 0.1g (saturated 0.0g)

Fiber 2.9g

Protein 0.5g

Cholesterol 0mg

Sodium 18mg

Calcium 9mg

Iron 0.7mg

1. Combine jícama and citrus sections in a medium bowl; set aside.

2. Combine sugar and lime juice in a small bowl, stirring until sugar
dissolves. Pour lime mixture over jícama mixture; sprinkle with
chopped mint, and toss gently. Yield: 4 servings (serving size: 1 cup).

quick tip: Jícama is a large root vegetable with a thin
brown skin and sweet taste. Its texture is similar to a
water chestnut.

Fresh Peach-Orange Salad

POINTS:

2

exchanges:

2 Fruit

per serving:

Calories 124
Carbohydrate 31.0g
Fat 0.4g (saturated 0.0g)
Fiber 5.4g
Protein 1.3g
Cholesterol 0mg
Sodium 5mg
Calcium 38mg
Iron 0.5mg

2	medium oranges
2	cups diced, peeled fresh peaches (about 2 large)
⅓	cup dried cherries
1	tablespoon sugar
½	teaspoon vanilla extract
½	teaspoon grated fresh ginger
4	Bibb lettuce leaves

1. Grate 1 teaspoon rind from orange; set aside. Peel oranges, and cut out sections over a medium bowl; squeeze membranes to extract juice. Reserve juice. Discard membranes.

2. Combine orange sections, reserved juice and rind, peaches, and next 4 ingredients. Serve on lettuce leaves. Yield: 4 servings (serving size: 1 lettuce leaf and ¾ cup peach mixture).

super food: You probably know that oranges are packed with vitamin C. But did you also know this citrus fruit is loaded with potassium and flavonoids? Flavonoids are a group of nutrients that may reduce cancer risk.

Orange and Romaine with Curry Dressing

¼ cup white balsamic vinegar

3 tablespoons honey

1 tablespoon olive oil

1½ teaspoons curry powder

¼ teaspoon crushed red pepper flakes

¼ teaspoon salt

3 cups torn romaine lettuce

1¼ cups sliced red onion

2 large oranges, peeled and cut crosswise into slices

1. Combine first 6 ingredients in a small bowl; stir well with a whisk. Set aside.

2. Arrange ¾ cup lettuce on each of 4 salad plates; top evenly with sliced onion and orange slices. Drizzle 2 tablespoons dressing over each salad. Serve immediately. Yield: 4 servings.

quick tip: Lettuces such as romaine are extremely low in calories and contain a fair amount of vitamin C. Cut your prep time by picking up packaged ready-to-eat lettuce in your grocer's produce department.

POINTS:

2

exchanges:

½ Starch

1 Vegetable

½ Fruit

½ Fat

per serving:

Calories 132

Carbohydrate 25.5g

Fat 3.7g (saturated 0.5g)

Fiber 4.5g

Protein 1.9g

Cholesterol 0mg

Sodium 152mg

Calcium 53mg

Iron 1.0mg

Fresh Pear Salad with Raspberry-Wine Vinaigrette

POINTS:

2

exchanges:

½ Starch

1 Vegetable

½ Fruit

½ Fat

per serving:

Calories 119

Carbohydrate 22.0g

Fat 3.1g (saturated 0.5g)

Fiber 2.5g

Protein 1.2g

Cholesterol 0mg

Sodium 123mg

Calcium 29mg

Iron 0.9mg

¼ cup raspberry wine vinegar
¼ cup dry white wine
3 tablespoons honey
1 tablespoon vegetable oil
¼ teaspoon salt
5 cups gourmet salad greens
2 red pears, thinly sliced

1. Combine first 5 ingredients in a small bowl; stir well with a whisk. Set aside.

2. Arrange 1 cup greens on each of 5 individual salad plates; top evenly with sliced pear. Spoon 2 tablespoons dressing over each salad; serve immediately. Yield: 5 servings.

quick tip: Gourmet salad greens are often called mesclun and are available in the produce department of your grocery store. If you aren't able to find this mix of greens, simply substitute romaine lettuce or fresh spinach.

Spring Greens with Strawberries and Honey-Watermelon Dressing photo, page 135

1 cup diced watermelon
1½ tablespoons honey
1 tablespoon raspberry wine vinegar
1 tablespoon vegetable oil
¼ teaspoon salt
5 cups gourmet salad greens
1¼ cups sliced fresh strawberries
½ cup thinly sliced red onion
⅓ cup sliced almonds, toasted
Freshly ground pepper

POINTS:
2

exchanges:
1 Vegetable
½ Fruit
1 Fat

per serving:
Calories 113
Carbohydrate 13.9g
Fat 6.1g (saturated 0.8g)
Fiber 2.9g
Protein 2.7g
Cholesterol 0mg
Sodium 124mg
Calcium 45mg
Iron 1.1mg

1. Combine first 5 ingredients in container of an electric blender; cover and process until smooth, stopping once to scrape down sides.

2. Place 1 cup greens on each of 5 individual salad plates. Top evenly with strawberries, red onion, and almonds. Drizzle 2 tablespoons dressing over each salad. Sprinkle with pepper. Serve immediately. Yield: 5 servings.

 quick tip: Store fresh strawberries in the refrigerator for two to three days. Wash them, and remove their green caps just before using.

Lemon-Dill White Bean Salad photo, page 133

POINTS:

2

exchanges:

1 Starch

½ Vegetable

½ Fat

per serving:

Calories 122

Carbohydrate 17.4g

Fat 3.9g (saturated 0.6g)

Fiber 4.0g

Protein 5.7g

Cholesterol 0mg

Sodium 541mg

Calcium 43mg

Iron 1.7mg

1   (16-ounce) can navy beans, rinsed and drained

½   cup chopped green onions

2   tablespoons chopped fresh dill

1   tablespoon extra-virgin olive oil

1   tablespoon lemon juice

½   teaspoon salt

8   slices tomato (about 1 large)

1   lemon, quartered (optional)

1. Combine first 6 ingredients in a medium bowl, tossing gently. Place 2 tomato slices on each of 4 individual salad plates; top each with ½ cup bean mixture. Serve with a lemon wedge, if desired. Yield: 4 servings.

 super food: Beans are a terrific source of folate, the nutrient that helps prevent certain birth defects. It also lowers homocysteine levels (high levels are linked to heart disease and heart attack).

Garlicky Bean and Spinach Salad

2¼ cups coarsely chopped spinach
1 (15-ounce) can navy beans, rinsed and drained
½ cup sliced red onion
1 tablespoon cider vinegar
1 tablespoon extra-virgin olive oil
1 garlic clove, minced
¼ teaspoon salt
⅛ teaspoon pepper

1. Combine first 3 ingredients in a large bowl. Combine vinegar and remaining 4 ingredients in a small bowl; add to bean mixture, tossing gently to coat. Serve immediately. Yield: 4 servings (serving size: 1 cup).

super food: Spinach offers a powerhouse of nutrients. It is loaded with folate, beta carotene, and vitamin C. Spinach also contains some of the highest levels of lutein of any vegetable. This phytochemical protects the eyes from harmful ultraviolet rays.

POINTS:

3

exchanges:
1 Starch
1 Vegetable
½ Very Lean Meat
½ Fat

per serving:
Calories 154
Carbohydrate 22.8g
Fat 3.9g (saturated 0.6g)
Fiber 6.1g
Protein 8.4g
Cholesterol 0mg
Sodium 478mg
Calcium 82mg
Iron 2.8mg

Gingered Beet and Spinach Salad

POINTS:
1

exchanges:
2 Vegetable
½ Fruit

per serving:
Calories 92
Carbohydrate 21.4g
Fat 0.4g (saturated 0.1g)
Fiber 5.9g
Protein 3.5g
Cholesterol 0mg
Sodium 290mg
Calcium 106mg
Iron 2.5mg

4   cups coarsely chopped fresh spinach
2   large oranges, peeled and sectioned
1   cup peeled and diced beet (about 2 medium)
3   tablespoons lime juice
1½ tablespoons sugar
1½ teaspoons grated fresh ginger
¼   teaspoon crushed red pepper flakes
¼   teaspoon salt

1. Combine spinach, orange sections, and beets in a large bowl; set aside.

2. Combine lime juice and remaining 4 ingredients in a small bowl; stir well with a whisk. Pour lime juice mixture over spinach mixture, tossing well. Let stand 5 minutes. Yield: 3 servings (serving size: 1 cup).

 quick tip: Beets are a good source of iron, fiber, and potassium. Peel the beets under running water to prevent them from staining your hands.

Shredded Apple Slaw

¼ cup light mayonnaise
1 tablespoon cider vinegar
1 to 1½ teaspoons sugar
¼ teaspoon salt
1 (8-ounce) Granny Smith apple, unpeeled
3 cups finely shredded cabbage

1. Combine first 4 ingredients in a small bowl, and stir until smooth with a whisk. Set aside.

2. Shred apple. Combine shredded apple and cabbage in a large bowl; add mayonnaise mixture, and toss gently to coat. Yield: 4 servings (serving size: ¾ cup).

super food: Eating an apple a day is a great way to increase your fiber intake and possibly prevent certain types of cancer.

POINTS:
2

exchanges:
1 Vegetable
½ Fruit
1 Fat

per serving:
Calories 84
Carbohydrate 12.1g
Fat 4.3g (saturated 1.0g)
Fiber 2.5g
Protein 0.9g
Cholesterol 5mg
Sodium 267mg
Calcium 28mg
Iron 0.4mg

Asian Peanut Slaw

POINTS:

2

exchanges:

½ Starch

1 Vegetable

1 Fat

2½ tablespoons cider vinegar

2½ tablespoons sugar

2 tablespoons low-sodium soy sauce

1 teaspoon grated fresh ginger

¼ cup unsalted peanuts, toasted

1½ cups shredded bok choy

1¼ cups thinly sliced red cabbage

per serving:

Calories 100

Carbohydrate 13.1g

Fat 4.6g (saturated 0.6g)

Fiber 1.7g

Protein 3.6g

Cholesterol 0mg

Sodium 264mg

Calcium 54mg

Iron 0.7mg

1. Combine first 4 ingredients in a small bowl; stir well with a whisk. Set aside.

2. Combine peanuts, bok choy, and cabbage in a medium bowl; add dressing, and toss gently to coat. Serve with a slotted spoon. Yield: 4 servings (serving size: ⅔ cup).

super food: This simple slaw is loaded with cruciferous vegetables such as bok choy and red cabbage, which may reduce the risk of cancer.

Yellow Pepper Slaw

1	yellow bell pepper, cut into ¼-inch-thick strips (about 1 cup)
½	cup shredded red cabbage
1	tablespoon cider vinegar
2	teaspoons honey
1	teaspoon low-sodium soy sauce
1	teaspoon sesame oil
½	teaspoon grated fresh ginger

POINTS:
1

exchanges:
1½ Vegetable

per serving:
Calories 46
Carbohydrate 8.2g
Fat 1.7g (saturated 0.2g)
Fiber 0.8g
Protein 0.8g
Cholesterol 0mg
Sodium 57mg
Calcium 15mg
Iron 0.4mg

1. Combine bell pepper and cabbage in a medium bowl; set aside.

2. Combine vinegar and remaining 4 ingredients in a small bowl; stir well with a whisk. Add to bell pepper mixture, and toss gently to coat. Yield: 3 servings (serving size: ½ cup).

super food: Move over orange juice—bell peppers are also an excellent source of the antioxidant vitamin C.

Creamy Green Pea Salad

POINTS:

1

exchanges:

2 Vegetable

½ Fat

per serving:

Calories 75

Carbohydrate 10.7g

Fat 2.3g (saturated 0.6g)

Fiber 3.4g

Protein 3.6g

Cholesterol 2mg

Sodium 299mg

Calcium 29mg

Iron 1.1mg

2   cups frozen green peas, thawed

1   cup finely chopped celery (about 3 ribs)

¼   cup finely chopped onion

2   tablespoons light mayonnaise

¾   teaspoon chopped fresh rosemary or ¼ teaspoon chopped dried
      rosemary

¼   teaspoon salt

¼   teaspoon freshly ground pepper

1. Combine all ingredients in a medium bowl, and toss gently to coat.
Serve immediately. Yield: 4 servings (serving size: ⅔ cup).

quick tip: Keep the prep time to a minimum by
thawing the peas while you chop the celery and onion.

**Lemon-Dill White
Bean Salad**
recipe, page 126

Greek Vegetable Rotini Salad
recipe, page 138

**Spring Greens with
Strawberries and Honey-
Watermelon Dressing**
recipe, page 125

Pineapple-Mango Salad
recipe, page 120

Couscous with Corn and Tomatoes

1½ cups fat-free vegetable broth

1 cup uncooked couscous

1 (11-ounce) can whole kernel corn, undrained

1½ cups halved grape tomatoes

⅔ cup minced fresh parsley

2 tablespoons lemon juice

1 tablespoon extra-virgin olive oil

1 garlic clove, minced

½ teaspoon salt

¼ teaspoon pepper

POINTS:

4

exchanges:

2 Starch

1 Vegetable

½ Fat

per serving:

Calories 188

Carbohydrate 36.5g

Fat 3.2g (saturated 0.4g)

Fiber 2.3g

Protein 5.8g

Cholesterol 0mg

Sodium 597mg

Calcium 15mg

Iron 1.4mg

1. Bring broth to a boil in a medium saucepan. Add couscous; stir well. Cover, remove from heat, and let stand 5 minutes.

2. Transfer couscous to a large bowl, and fluff with a fork. Add corn and remaining 7 ingredients; toss well. Yield: 6 cups (serving size: 1 cup).

 quick tip: Grape tomatoes are slightly smaller than cherry tomatoes and are ideal in salads because they aren't watery like larger tomatoes. They also are great to keep on hand for a simple, nutritious snack.

Greek Vegetable Rotini Salad photo, page 134

POINTS:

2

exchanges:

1 Starch

1 Vegetable

½ Fat

per serving:

Calories 113

Carbohydrate 19.2g

Fat 2.5g (saturated 1.1g)

Fiber 1.4g

Protein 3.8g

Cholesterol 5mg

Sodium 154mg

Calcium 43mg

Iron 1.3mg

4   ounces tricolored rotini, uncooked (2 cups uncooked pasta)

1⅓ cups seeded and chopped tomato (about 1 large)

¼   cup finely chopped red onion

⅔   cup thinly sliced green bell pepper (about 1 small)

12   kalamata olives

⅓   cup (1⅓ ounces) crumbled tomato-basil feta cheese

2   tablespoons chopped fresh basil

¼   teaspoon freshly ground pepper

3   tablespoons fat-free balsamic vinaigrette

1. Cook pasta according to package directions, omitting salt and fat; drain. Rinse pasta under cold water; drain and set aside.

2. Combine tomato, onion, and bell pepper; add to pasta. Stir in olives and next 3 ingredients. Add vinaigrette, and toss gently to coat. Cover and chill 1 hour. Yield: 6 servings (serving size: ¾ cup).

super food: If you increase the variety of foods you eat, you'll create a healthy diet. This pasta salad is loaded with plenty of different good-for-you foods with an abundance of flavors.

Sandwiches
&
Soups

Mediterranean Hummus Sandwiches

POINTS:

6

exchanges:

3 Starch

1 Vegetable

½ Lean Meat

1 Fat

per serving:

Calories 310

Carbohydrate 49.3g

Fat 8.5g (saturated 1.3g)

Fiber 7.9g

Protein 12.3g

Cholesterol 5mg

Sodium 769mg

Calcium 78mg

Iron 4.0mg

½ cup hummus with roasted red peppers

2 (6-inch) whole wheat pita bread rounds, cut in half

2 tablespoons (½ ounce) crumbled garlic-and-herb feta cheese

1 small cucumber, thinly sliced

1 large plum tomato, thinly sliced

2 pepperoncini peppers, thinly sliced

1. Spread 2 tablespoons hummus inside each pita half; sprinkle each half evenly with feta cheese. Arrange cucumber and tomato in pita halves; top with peppers. Yield: 2 servings (serving size: 2 pita halves).

quick tip: Hummus, which is made from chickpeas (garbanzo beans), is a great source of fiber. It's also an alternate source of protein. Look for hummus in the deli department of your grocery store.

prep: 13 minutes   chill: 1 hour   cook: 16 minutes

Veggie Burgers photo, page 154

1   (19-ounce) can chickpeas (garbanzo beans), rinsed and drained
1   cup sliced green onions
⅔   cup (2⅔ ounces) freshly grated Parmesan cheese
½   teaspoon salt
1   (8-ounce) can cut green beans, drained
1   tablespoon lemon pepper seasoning
1   garlic clove, minced
1   cup cooked brown rice
Cooking spray
6   whole wheat hamburger buns
Ketchup, mustard, pickles, onion slices, tomato slices, lettuce, alfalfa
     sprouts (optional)

POINTS:
5

exchanges:
2½ Starch
1 Vegetable
1 Medium-Fat Meat

per serving:
Calories 269
Carbohydrate 45.9g
Fat 5.7g (saturated 2.3g)
Fiber 8.2g
Protein 14.8g
Cholesterol 9mg
Sodium 962mg
Calcium 239mg
Iron 3.0mg

1. Combine first 8 ingredients in a food processor bowl. Pulse 3 to 4 times or until chopped. Transfer mixture to a large bowl, and stir in rice. Cover and chill mixture at least 1 hour.

2. Shape vegetable mixture into 6 bun-size patties. Heat a large nonstick skillet over medium heat until hot. Coat patties with cooking spray. Cook patties, in batches, if necessary, in skillet over medium heat 8 minutes on each side or until browned. Transfer patties to a plate, and let cool slightly. Serve patties on whole wheat buns with condiments, if desired. Yield: 6 servings.

cooking secret: These burgers are a great use for leftover cooked brown rice. They're also ideal to keep on hand for a quick meal. Once the vegetable mixture is shaped into patties, you can freeze them in a freezer-safe container for up to three weeks.

Eggplant on French Bread with Tomato-Kalamata Salsa

POINTS:

5

exchanges:

1 Starch

1½ Vegetable

1 Lean Meat

1 Fat

per serving:

Calories 223

Carbohydrate 24.4g

Fat 9.6g (saturated 3.7g)

Fiber 3.5g

Protein 11.0g

Cholesterol 16mg

Sodium 451mg

Calcium 231mg

Iron 1.8mg

1   large tomato, seeded and chopped

12   kalamata olives, pitted and chopped

⅓   cup chopped fresh basil leaves

1½ teaspoons red wine vinegar

4   (1-ounce) diagonally cut slices French bread (about ¾ inch thick)

4   (½-inch-thick) diagonally cut slices unpeeled eggplant

1   tablespoon olive oil

1   cup (4 ounces) shredded part-skim mozzarella cheese

1. Combine first 4 ingredients in a medium bowl; toss well. Set aside.

2. Arrange bread, cut side up, on an ungreased baking sheet. Broil 5½ inches from heat 3 minutes or until lightly toasted.

3. Arrange eggplant in a single layer on a baking sheet. Brush eggplant evenly with olive oil. Broil 3 inches from heat 2 minutes on each side or until golden.

4. Top each bread slice with 2 tablespoons olive mixture, 1 eggplant slice, 2 additional tablespoons olive mixture, and ¼ cup cheese. Broil 5 inches from heat 1½ minutes or until lightly browned. Allow to stand 3 minutes. Yield: 4 servings.

Sweet Pepper Sourdough Melts photo, page 156

1   (8-ounce) flute sourdough bread, cut in half lengthwise and then
      crosswise
1   tablespoon plus 1 teaspoon commercial pesto
1   (16-ounce) package frozen pepper stir-fry, thawed and drained
      (such as Birds Eye)
Olive-oil flavored cooking spray
2   garlic cloves, minced
¼   teaspoon salt
¼   teaspoon pepper
1   cup (4 ounces) shredded part-skim mozzarella cheese

POINTS:
6

exchanges:
2 Starch
2 Vegetable
½ Medium-Fat Meat
1 Fat

per serving:
Calories 305
Carbohydrate 40.6g
Fat 9.2g (saturated 3.8g)
Fiber 4.7g
Protein 14.4g
Cholesterol 17mg
Sodium 730mg
Calcium 271mg
Iron 2.3mg

1. Place bread, cut side up, on an ungreased baking sheet. Broil 5½
inches from heat 3 minutes or until lightly toasted. Spread evenly with
pesto; set aside.

2. Heat a large nonstick skillet over medium-high heat until hot. Coat
peppers with cooking spray. Cook pepper stir-fry, garlic, salt, and pepper 3 minutes, stirring constantly. Spoon about ½ cup pepper mixture
over each toasted bread portion; top each with ¼ cup cheese. Broil 3
additional minutes or until cheese melts. Yield: 4 servings.

super food: Frozen vegetables are just as nutritious as their
fresh counterparts—just watch out for those with cheese
and butter sauces.

Asian Beef and Spinach Wraps

POINTS:

9

exchanges:

2 Starch
1 Vegetable
1 Fruit
3½ Lean Meat

per serving:

Calories 439
Carbohydrate 50.8g
Fat 11.0g (saturated 3.1g)
Fiber 3.6g
Protein 32.3g
Cholesterol 76mg
Sodium 813mg
Calcium 110mg
Iron 5.8mg

1   pound top sirloin steak
¼   cup reduced-sodium soy sauce
2   teaspoons sugar
1   tablespoon cornstarch
2   teaspoons minced fresh ginger
1   garlic clove, minced
¼   teaspoon crushed red pepper flakes
1   teaspoon dark sesame oil
2   cups thinly sliced red onion (about 1 large)
4   cups trimmed fresh spinach
4   (10-inch) flour tortillas
1   (11-ounce) can mandarin oranges, drained

1. Cut steak diagonally across grain into ¼-inch-thick slices. Set aside. Combine soy sauce and next 5 ingredients in a small bowl, stirring until cornstarch dissolves. Add steak; stir well. Set aside.

2. Heat sesame oil in a large nonstick skillet over medium-high heat; add onion, and cook, stirring constantly, until tender. Add spinach to onion, and cook, stirring constantly, just until spinach wilts. Set aside, and keep warm.

3. Add steak mixture to skillet, and cook 3 to 4 minutes, stirring constantly.

4. Wrap tortillas in wax paper or damp paper towels, and microwave at HIGH 20 seconds or until warm.

5. Top each tortilla evenly with spinach mixture, steak mixture, and mandarin oranges. Roll up, and slice in half crosswise, securing each half with a wooden pick. Yield: 4 servings (serving size: 2 tortilla halves).

 meal idea: Serve these main-dish sandwiches with Pineapple-Mint Ice (page 38).

Chicken Wrap with Chipotle Sour Cream

½   to 1 chipotle pepper in adobo sauce, drained, seeded, and finely
      chopped
½   cup reduced-fat sour cream
3   cups seeded and finely chopped tomato (about 2 medium)
¼   teaspoon salt
1   pound skinned, boned chicken breast halves
1   teaspoon ground cumin
½   teaspoon black pepper
Cooking spray
4   (8-inch) flour tortillas
4   romaine lettuce leaves
1   lime, cut into wedges (optional)

POINTS:

7

exchanges:

1½ Starch
1½ Vegetable
3½ Lean Meat

per serving:

Calories 357
Carbohydrate 32.5g
Fat 10.5g (saturated 3.7g)
Fiber 3.1g
Protein 32.4g
Cholesterol 84mg
Sodium 471mg
Calcium 116mg
Iron 3.5mg

1. Combine chipotle pepper and sour cream in a small bowl; set aside.
Combine tomato and salt in a medium bowl; set aside.

2. Sprinkle both sides of chicken with cumin and black pepper. Place a
large nonstick skillet over high heat until hot; coat with cooking spray. Add
chicken, and cook 1 minute on each side. Reduce heat to medium, and
cook 3 to 4 minutes on each side or until done. Remove from skillet, and
let stand 5 minutes.

3. Slice chicken diagonally across grain into thin strips. Wrap tortillas in
wax paper or damp paper towels, and microwave at HIGH 20 seconds
or until warm.

4. Spoon 2 tablespoons sour cream mixture down the center of each
tortilla; top each with a lettuce leaf. Divide chicken evenly over lettuce;
sprinkle with tomato. Squeeze lime over tomato, if desired. Roll up, and
slice in half crosswise, securing each half with a wooden pick. Yield: 4
servings (serving size: 2 tortilla halves).

Chicken Salad Sandwiches

POINTS:

7

exchanges:

2½ Starch

½ Fruit

2½ Lean Meat

per serving:

Calories 364

Carbohydrate 43.6g

Fat 10.4g (saturated 1.6g)

Fiber 8.4g

Protein 26.2g

Cholesterol 53mg

Sodium 601mg

Calcium 38mg

Iron 3.0mg

1½ cups chopped cooked chicken breast

2 cups chopped unpeeled Red Delicious apple (about 1 large)

¼ cup minced red onion

¼ cup light mayonnaise

½ teaspoon curry powder

½ teaspoon sugar

¼ teaspoon salt

⅛ teaspoon pepper

½ cup chopped red bell pepper

8 (1.2-ounce) slices whole wheat bread

1. Combine first 9 ingredients in a large bowl. Spread 1 cup chicken mixture onto each of 4 bread slices. Top with remaining bread slices. Yield: 4 servings.

quick tip: This traditional chicken salad sandwich gets a nutritious boost with the addition of fiber-rich chopped apple and bell pepper. Serve these hearty sandwiches with cups of vegetable soup.

Smoked Turkey and Avocado Bagels

½   pound smoked turkey, finely chopped

⅓   cup chopped avocado (about ½ avocado)

½   teaspoon lemon juice

⅓   cup finely shredded carrot

2   tablespoons creamy mustard blend (such as Dijonnaise)

⅛   teaspoon pepper

2   fresh poppy seed bagels, halved and toasted

½   medium red onion, sliced and separated into rings

¼   cup alfalfa sprouts (about ½ pint)

POINTS:

6

exchanges:

2 Starch

1 Vegetable

1 Lean Meat

per serving:

Calories 312

Carbohydrate 37.5g

Fat 4.1g (saturated 0.8g)

Fiber 3.0g

Protein 16.8g

Cholesterol 24mg

Sodium 925mg

Calcium 60mg

Iron 2.7mg

1. Combine first 6 ingredients in a large bowl. Spread ½ cup turkey mixture on top of each bagel half. Top bagels evenly with onion rings and alfalfa sprouts. Yield: 4 servings (serving size: 1 bagel half).

quick tip: Bagels are a healthy alternative to some high-fat breads, but make sure you watch portion sizes. Look for bagels that are about the size of the palm of your hand. Some bakery bagels can add up to four bread servings.

Turkey Pepperoni-Stuffed Pitas

POINTS:
5

exchanges:
2½ Starch
1 Vegetable
½ Medium-Fat Meat
½ Fat

per serving:
Calories 279
Carbohydrate 42.4g
Fat 6.8g (saturated 3.1g)
Fiber 6.2g
Protein 14.3g
Cholesterol 31mg
Sodium 841mg
Calcium 109mg
Iron 3.3mg

4   cups torn romaine lettuce
32 slices turkey pepperoni, cut in half
1   small zucchini, cut into 2-inch strips
½   cup thinly sliced red onion
2   tablespoons fat-free Ranch-style dressing
¼   teaspoon pepper
½   cup (2 ounces) crumbled feta cheese with basil and sun-dried
      tomatoes
4   whole wheat pita bread rounds, cut in half

1. Combine first 6 ingredients in a large bowl. Stir in feta cheese.

2. Wrap pita halves in damp paper towels, and microwave at HIGH 20
seconds. Spoon about ¾ cup lettuce mixture into each pita half.
Yield: 4 servings (serving size: 2 pita halves).

quick tip: For a slightly heartier sandwich with even more
fiber, omit the zucchini and add one 19-ounce can chickpeas (garbanzo beans), rinsed and drained.

Tropical Melon Soup photo, page 155

2   cups chopped fresh cantaloupe
1½ cups chopped fresh mango (about 2 medium)
1   tablespoon lemon juice
½   teaspoon almond extract
1   cup fat-free half-and-half
¼   cup cream of coconut
1   tablespoon plus 1 teaspoon flaked coconut, toasted

1. Combine first 6 ingredients in container of an electric blender. Cover and process until smooth, stopping once to scrape down sides. Cover and chill 1 hour.

2. To serve, ladle 1 cup soup into each of 4 individual serving bowls; sprinkle each with 1 teaspoon toasted coconut. Yield: 4 servings.

super food: This simple dessert soup is brimming with the cancer-fighting antioxidant, beta-carotene. This plant pigment is not only a powerful nutrient, but it also gives cantaloupe and mango their characteristic color.

POINTS:

3

exchanges:

1½ Fruit
1 Fat

per serving:

Calories 143
Carbohydrate 25.3g
Fat 4.2g (saturated 3.5g)
Fiber 2.3g
Protein 1.7g
Cholesterol 0mg
Sodium 53mg
Calcium 38mg
Iron 0.4mg

Creamy Peach Soup with Raspberry Coulis

POINTS:

4

exchanges:

2 Starch

1½ Fruit

per serving:

Calories 218

Carbohydrate 50.2g

Fat 0.6g (saturated 0.4g)

Fiber 2.6g

Protein 3.3g

Cholesterol 3mg

Sodium 45mg

Calcium 94mg

Iron 0.0mg

1   (14-ounce) package frozen unsweetened raspberries, thawed
2   tablespoons powdered sugar
¼   teaspoon almond extract
1¾ cups ginger ale, divided
1   (16-ounce) package frozen unsweetened peaches, thawed
1   (8-ounce) carton vanilla low-fat yogurt
½   cup frozen white grape juice concentrate

1. Add first 3 ingredients and ½ cup ginger ale to food processor bowl; puree until smooth. Cover and chill.

2. Pour raspberry mixture through a fine wire-mesh strainer into a small bowl. Use a rubber spatula against sides of strainer to extract juice; discard seeds. Cover and chill.

3. Place peaches, yogurt, and grape juice concentrate in food processor bowl; puree until smooth. Cover and chill 1 hour.

4. Add remaining 1¼ cups ginger ale to peach mixture just before serving, stirring well. To serve, ladle about 1 cup peach mixture into each of 5 individual serving bowls; drizzle each with ¼ cup raspberry coulis. Serve immediately. Yield: 5 servings.

quick tip: Swirl the raspberry coulis into the Peach Soup for an attractive presentation.

Chilled Strawberry-Ginger Soup

1   (16-ounce) package frozen unsweetened strawberries, partially
       thawed
1   (15-ounce) can pear halves in juice, undrained
½   cup frozen orange juice concentrate
¼   cup honey
1   tablespoon grated fresh ginger

1. Combine all ingredients in container of an electric blender. Cover
and process until smooth, stopping once to scrape down sides. Cover
and chill 1 hour. Yield: 6 servings (serving size: ¾ cup).

 quick tip: If you don't have time to peel, chop, or slice raw
fruits and vegetables, reach for frozen and canned foods.
For example, you can enjoy this quick fruit soup year-round
with convenient frozen berries and canned pears.

POINTS:
3

exchanges:
½ Starch
2 Fruit

per serving:
Calories 143
Carbohydrate 36.8g
Fat 0.2g (saturated 0.0g)
Fiber 1.4g
Protein 1.2g
Cholesterol 0mg
Sodium 6mg
Calcium 27mg
Iron 0.9mg

Gazpacho photo, facing page

POINTS:
2

exchanges:
3 Vegetable

per serving:
Calories 83
Carbohydrate 15.3g
Fat 1.5g (saturated 0.2g)
Fiber 1.3g
Protein 2.6g
Cholesterol 0mg
Sodium 804mg
Calcium 33mg
Iron 1.3mg

1   (14½-ounce) can diced tomatoes with garlic and onions,
       undrained and chilled
1   cup vegetable juice, chilled
¾   cup peeled, seeded, and coarsely chopped cucumber
½   cup chopped green bell pepper
⅓   cup chopped green onions
1   tablespoon red wine vinegar
1   teaspoon olive oil
1   garlic clove, minced
⅛   teaspoon hot sauce
¼   teaspoon salt
⅛   teaspoon freshly ground pepper
12 fat-free herb-seasoned croutons (such as Mrs. Cubbison's)

1. Combine first 11 ingredients in a large bowl. Cover and chill 1 hour.

2. To serve, ladle 1 cup soup into each of 4 individual serving bowls.
Top each with 3 croutons. Yield: 4 servings.

super food: This refreshing chilled soup is loaded with good-
for-you foods such as canned tomatoes and tomato juice.
Tomato products contain the nutrient lycopene, which may
help fight certain types of cancer.

Veggie Burgers
recipe, page 141

Tropical Melon Soup
recipe, page 149

**Sweet Pepper
Sourdough Melts**
recipe, page 143

Italian Bean Soup

Cooking spray

1   cup chopped green bell pepper (about 1 large)

1   cup chopped onion

2   (16-ounce) cans navy beans, rinsed and drained

1   (14½-ounce) can fat-free, reduced-sodium chicken broth

1   (14½-ounce) can diced Italian-style tomatoes, undrained

1   tablespoon commercial pesto

POINTS:

4

exchanges:

2 Starch

2 Vegetable

½ Very Lean Meat

per serving:

Calories 228

Carbohydrate 39.6g

Fat 2.8g (saturated 0.5g)

Fiber 7.2g

Protein 11.9g

Cholesterol 0mg

Sodium 1223mg

Calcium 162mg

Iron 4.7mg

1. Heat a Dutch oven coated with cooking spray over medium-high heat until hot. Add bell pepper and onion; cook 8 minutes or until onion is tender.

2. Add beans and remaining 3 ingredients. Bring to a boil, reduce heat, and simmer, uncovered, 10 minutes. Yield: 4 servings (serving size: 1½ cups).

 meal idea: Beans are a great source of cholesterol-lowering soluble fiber. Serve this heart-healthy soup with soft garlic breadsticks and a simple tossed salad with fat-free Italian dressing.

Southwestern Corn and Red Pepper Soup photo, page 1

POINTS:

3

exchanges:

2 Starch

½ Lean Meat

per serving:

Calories 184

Carbohydrate 30.6g

Fat 3.4g (saturated 1.7g)

Fiber 3.7g

Protein 10.7g

Cholesterol 11mg

Sodium 699mg

Calcium 248mg

Iron 1.2mg

1	(16-ounce) package frozen whole-kernel corn, thawed
¾	cup chopped red bell pepper (about 1 medium)
¾	cup chopped green onions, divided
1	(14½-ounce) can fat-free, reduced-sodium chicken broth
1	(5-ounce) can fat-free evaporated milk
½	cup (2 ounces) shredded reduced-fat sharp Cheddar cheese
½	teaspoon salt
⅛	teaspoon ground red pepper

Freshly ground black pepper

1. Cook corn, bell pepper, and ½ cup chopped green onions in a Dutch oven over medium-high heat 2 minutes. Add chicken broth and evaporated milk. Bring to a boil; cover, reduce heat, and simmer 15 minutes, stirring occasionally.

2. Puree 1 cup of corn mixture in an electric blender until smooth; return mixture to Dutch oven. Stir in cheese, salt, and ground red pepper.

3. To serve, ladle 1¼ cups soup into each of 4 individual serving bowls. Sprinkle each with 1 tablespoon green onions and black pepper. Yield: 4 servings.

 meal idea: Pick up a package of jalapeño cornbread mix and two fresh oranges to round out the meal. Bake the cornsticks and cut the oranges into wedges while the soup simmers.

Portobello Mushroom Soup

1   tablespoon light stick butter

2   portobello mushroom caps, sliced and halved (about 8 ounces)

¾   cup chopped green onions

2   tablespoons all-purpose flour

1   (14½-ounce) can fat-free, reduced-sodium chicken broth

½   teaspoon salt

¼   teaspoon pepper

½   cup low-fat sour cream

½   cup fat-free half-and-half

POINTS:

3

exchanges:

½ Starch

1 Vegetable

1 Fat

per serving:

Calories 117

Carbohydrate 12.0g

Fat 5.4g (saturated 3.2g)

Fiber 1.3g

Protein 3.0g

Cholesterol 17mg

Sodium 602mg

Calcium 68mg

Iron 1.2mg

1. Melt butter in a Dutch oven over medium-high heat. Add mushrooms, and cook, stirring constantly, 3 to 5 minutes or until tender. Add green onions, and cook 2 minutes.

2. Whisk together flour, broth, salt, and pepper in a medium bowl; add to mushroom mixture, stirring well to combine. Bring to a boil, and cook, uncovered, 1 minute. Remove from heat.

3. Combine sour cream and half-and-half in a small bowl, stirring until well blended. Stir into mushroom mixture, and cook, uncovered, over low heat, stirring often, 12 minutes or until thoroughly heated. Yield: 4 servings (serving size: 1 cup)

quick tip: Portobello mushrooms are prized for their dense, meaty texture. If you buy whole portobellos rather than caps, remove the tough stems before using the mushrooms.

Creamy Pumpkin Soup

POINTS:
2

exchanges:
1 Starch
1 Vegetable

per serving:
Calories 114
Carbohydrate 18.5g
Fat 1.5g (saturated 1.0g)
Fiber 3.8g
Protein 1.2g
Cholesterol 4mg
Sodium 567mg
Calcium 85mg
Iron 1.3mg

1	tablespoon light stick butter
½	cup chopped onion
1	(15-ounce) can unsweetened pumpkin
¾	teaspoon salt
¼	teaspoon ground cinnamon
¼	teaspoon ground nutmeg
⅛	teaspoon pepper
1	tablespoon brown sugar
1	cup fat-free, reduced-sodium chicken broth
1¾	cups fat-free half-and-half

1. Melt butter in a large saucepan over medium heat; add onion, and cook 5 minutes or until tender, stirring constantly. Add pumpkin and remaining ingredients, stirring well with a whisk. Bring to a boil; cover, reduce heat, and simmer 5 minutes.

2. Puree mixture, in batches, in an electric blender. Return to saucepan, and cook until thoroughly heated. Yield: 5 servings (serving size: 1 cup).

 meal idea: Serve this savory soup with Maple-Glazed Apples (page 164).

Summer Squash Soup

1   tablespoon light stick butter

1½ pounds fresh yellow squash, sliced and cut in half (about 4½ cups)

1   cup chopped Vidalia or other sweet onion

1   (14½-ounce) can fat-free, reduced-sodium chicken broth

½   cup 2% reduced-fat milk

1½ teaspoons chopped fresh thyme

½   teaspoon salt

⅛   teaspoon pepper

2   tablespoons freshly grated Parmesan cheese

POINTS:

1

exchanges:

2 Vegetable

½ Fat

per serving:

Calories 86

Carbohydrate 11.1g

Fat 3.1g (saturated 1.8g)

Fiber 3.0g

Protein 4.1g

Cholesterol 9mg

Sodium 614mg

Calcium 101mg

Iron 0.8mg

1. Melt butter in a large saucepan over medium heat; add squash and onion. Cover and cook 13 minutes or until squash and onion are very tender.

2. Transfer squash mixture to a food processor bowl; puree until smooth. Return squash mixture to saucepan. Stir in broth and next 4 ingredients; cook, uncovered, over low heat until thoroughly heated.

3. To serve, ladle 1 cup soup into each of 4 individual serving bowls, and top evenly with Parmesan cheese. Yield: 4 servings.

quick tip: This simple soup makes use of two of summer's finest fresh vegetables: yellow squash and Vidalia onions.

New England Clam Chowder

POINTS:

2

exchanges:

½ Starch
½ Vegetable
½ Very Lean Meat

per serving:

Calories 143
Carbohydrate 25.8g
Fat 0.8g (saturated 0.4g)
Fiber 2.7g
Protein 7.0g
Cholesterol 18mg
Sodium 509mg
Calcium 53mg
Iron 1.8mg

2	teaspoons light stick butter
3¼	cups unpeeled and diced round red potatoes (about 3 medium)
1½	cups chopped onion (about 1 medium)
1	cup chopped celery (about 2 stalks)
1	cup chopped carrot (about 2½ medium)
¼	teaspoon pepper
3	(8-ounce) bottles clam juice, divided
2	tablespoons all-purpose flour
2	(6.5-ounce) cans minced clams, undrained
¾	cup fat-free half-and-half

1. Melt butter in a Dutch oven over medium heat. Add potato and next 4 ingredients. Cover and cook over medium heat, stirring occasionally, 10 minutes (do not brown).

2. Whisk together ½ cup clam juice and flour in a small bowl; add to vegetables, stirring gently. Stir in remaining clam juice. Bring to a boil; reduce heat, and simmer, uncovered, 25 minutes or until vegetables are tender. Stir in clams and half-and-half. Yield: 7 servings (serving size: 1 cup).

meal idea: We gave this chowder a high rating for its rich taste and creamy texture. Serve it with a tossed salad and crackers.

Side
Dishes

Maple-Glazed Apples

POINTS:

4

exchanges:

1 Starch
1½ Fruit
1 Fat

per serving:

Calories 214
Carbohydrate 41.0g
Fat 5.8g (saturated 0.5g)
Fiber 4.5g
Protein 1.6g
Cholesterol 0mg
Sodium 5mg
Calcium 38mg
Iron 0.9mg

⅓ cup pure maple syrup
½ teaspoon ground cinnamon
¼ teaspoon ground allspice
⅓ cup dried cherries
½ teaspoon vanilla extract
¼ cup chopped pecans
Cooking spray
4   Golden Delicious apples, peeled, cored, and cut into wedges

1. Combine first 6 ingredients in a small bowl; set aside.

2. Coat a large nonstick skillet with cooking spray; add apple. Pour syrup mixture over apple; stir well to coat completely. Cover and cook over medium heat, 30 minutes or until apples are tender, stirring occasionally. Yield: 4 servings (serving size: ⅔ cup).

super food: An apple a day may keep cancer at bay, according to recent research. Apples contain antioxidant nutrients that may help reduce cancer risk. They also are an excellent source of fiber, which has been found to reduce cholesterol and may prevent certain types of cancer.

Asparagus Spears with Garlic Aïoli
photo, page 176

⅓ cup plain low-fat yogurt

1½ tablespoons light mayonnaise

1 teaspoon Dijon mustard

2 garlic cloves, minced

⅛ teaspoon salt

1 pound fresh asparagus

Paprika

POINTS:

1

exchanges:

1 Vegetable

½ Fat

per serving:

Calories 51

Carbohydrate 5.8g

Fat 2.2g (saturated 0.6g)

Fiber 0.8g

Protein 3.3g

Cholesterol 3mg

Sodium 175mg

Calcium 56mg

Iron 0.6mg

1. Combine first 5 ingredients in a small bowl, stirring well with a whisk. Set aside.

2. Snap off tough ends of asparagus; remove scales from stalks with a vegetable peeler, if desired.

3. Place asparagus spears in a large skillet; add water to cover. Bring to a boil over high heat; cover, reduce heat, and simmer 3 minutes or until asparagus is crisp-tender. Plunge asparagus into cold water to stop the cooking process; drain. Place asparagus on a serving platter; spoon yogurt mixture over asparagus. Sprinkle with paprika. Yield: 4 servings.

quick tip: When shopping for asparagus, choose firm, pencil-thin spears that are uniform in size with tightly closed bright-green and lavender-tinted tips. Uniformity in size and shape is important for even cooking.

Green Beans Gremolata

POINTS:

0

exchanges:

1½ Vegetable

per serving:

Calories 43

Carbohydrate 6.8g

Fat 1.8g (saturated 1.1g)

Fiber 2.6g

Protein 1.9g

Cholesterol 5mg

Sodium 168mg

Calcium 46mg

Iron 0.9mg

1   (14-ounce) package frozen whole green beans

1   tablespoon light stick butter, softened

2   tablespoons finely chopped fresh flat-leaf parsley

1   tablespoon grated lemon rind

2   garlic cloves, minced

¼   teaspoon salt

⅛   teaspoon pepper

1. Steam beans, covered, 7 minutes or until crisp-tender. Transfer to a large serving bowl. Add butter and remaining 5 ingredients, and toss gently. Yield: 4 servings (serving size: ¾ cup).

quick tip: Frozen green beans are a great staple vegetable to keep on hand for a quick, nutritious side dish.

Gingered Orange Beets photo, page 175

6   medium beets, peeled and sliced into ¼-inch-thick slices (about 2 pounds)
2   teaspoons olive oil
½   teaspoon salt
¼   teaspoon pepper
1½ teaspoons grated fresh ginger
¼   cup orange marmalade
1   tablespoon orange juice

POINTS:
2

exchanges:
1 Starch
3 Vegetable
½ Fat

per serving:
Calories 147
Carbohydrate 30.5g
Fat 2.6g (saturated 0.4g)
Fiber 4.9g
Protein 2.9g
Cholesterol 0mg
Sodium 437mg
Calcium 37mg
Iron 1.5mg

1. Combine first 4 ingredients in a large bowl; toss gently. Set aside.

2. Combine ginger, marmalade, and orange juice in a small bowl, stirring well. Set aside.

3. Place beets in a single layer in a shallow roasting pan or jellyroll pan. Bake at 450° for 12 minutes.

4. Remove beets from oven, and brush with ginger-orange mixture. Return to oven, and bake 10 to 12 additional minutes or until tender. Yield: 4 servings (serving size: ½ cup).

quick tip: Beets have the highest sugar content of any vegetable. Roasting beets caramelizes the sugar, adding a depth of flavor. This simple ginger-orange glaze enhances beets' natural sweet flavor.

Broccoli with Garlic and Lemon Pepper Sauce

POINTS:

2

exchanges:

2 Vegetable

1 Fat

per serving:

Calories 86

Carbohydrate 8.9g

Fat 5.2g (saturated 3.1g)

Fiber 3.1g

Protein 4.7g

Cholesterol 15mg

Sodium 372mg

Calcium 61mg

Iron 1.3mg

1   pound fresh broccoli

3   tablespoons light stick butter

2   to 3 garlic cloves, minced

3   tablespoons lemon juice

1½ tablespoons white wine Worcestershire sauce

⅓   cup water

1   tablespoon Dijon mustard

¼   teaspoon salt

⅛   teaspoon crushed red pepper flakes

1. Steam broccoli, covered, 7 minutes or until crisp-tender. Transfer to a serving bowl, and keep warm.

2. Melt butter in a large nonstick skillet over medium-high heat; add garlic. Cook garlic, stirring constantly, 1 minute or until golden. Add lemon juice and remaining 5 ingredients; bring to a boil. Pour over broccoli; toss gently. Serve immediately. Yield: 4 servings.

super food: Broccoli is one of the best foods you can put on your plate. Phytochemicals in broccoli help to protect your cells' DNA from harmful free radicals.

Sweet-and-Sour Brussels Sprouts with Bacon photo, page 174

1¼ pounds fresh Brussels sprouts, trimmed and halved lengthwise
3   slices lower sodium bacon
2   tablespoons dark brown sugar
3   tablespoons white wine vinegar
½   teaspoon salt
¼   teaspoon pepper

POINTS:

1

exchanges:

2 Vegetable
½ Fat

per serving:

Calories 67
Carbohydrate 10.2g
Fat 2.0g (saturated 0.7g)
Fiber 3.5g
Protein 4.0g
Cholesterol 4mg
Sodium 275mg
Calcium 37mg
Iron 1.2mg

1. Place Brussels sprouts in a large nonstick skillet; add water to cover. Bring to a boil; reduce heat, and simmer, uncovered, 5 minutes. Drain; cover and keep warm. Set aside.

2. Cook bacon in a large nonstick skillet over medium heat until crisp. Remove bacon from skillet; crumble and set aside. Pour excess fat from skillet, reserving any brown bits; discard fat.

3. Add sugar, vinegar, salt, and pepper to skillet, stirring to dissolve sugar. Return Brussels sprouts to skillet, and cook until thoroughly heated. Stir in reserved bacon. Yield: 6 servings (serving size: ⅔ cup).

quick tip: Look for small Brussels sprouts with bright green leaves and compact heads. They are the most tender.

Sugared Carrots

POINTS:
1

exchanges:
2 Vegetable

per serving:
Calories 71
Carbohydrate 13.9g
Fat 1.7g (saturated 1.1g)
Fiber 2.8g
Protein 1.2g
Cholesterol 5mg
Sodium 125mg
Calcium 29mg
Iron 0.6mg

1   pound carrots, scraped and cut into ⅛-inch-thick diagonal slices
2   tablespoons brown sugar
1   tablespoon light stick butter, melted
¼   teaspoon ground nutmeg
¼   teaspoon vanilla extract
⅛   teaspoon salt

1. Steam carrot, covered, 6 minutes or until crisp-tender. Transfer to a serving bowl, and keep warm.

2. Combine brown sugar and remaining 4 ingredients in a small bowl. Drizzle over carrot; toss well. Yield: 4 servings (serving size: ½ cup).

super food: Carrots are a nutritious powerhouse, prized for the beta-carotene and lutein they contain. Beta-carotene protects the body's cells, while lutein helps preserve eyesight.

Curried Cauliflower

2	teaspoons light stick butter
1	cup chopped onion
1	garlic clove
1	(1-inch) piece fresh ginger, minced
4	cups fresh cauliflower flowerets
½	cup water
1½	teaspoons curry powder
½	teaspoon salt

POINTS:

0

exchanges:

2 Vegetable

per serving:

Calories 50
Carbohydrate 8.9g
Fat 1.4g (saturated 0.7g)
Fiber 3.4g
Protein 2.7g
Cholesterol 3mg
Sodium 337mg
Calcium 35mg
Iron 0.8mg

1. Melt butter in a large nonstick skillet over medium-high heat. Add onion, garlic, and ginger, and cook, stirring constantly, 5 minutes. Add cauliflower and remaining 3 ingredients. Bring to a boil; cover, reduce heat, and simmer 7 to 8 minutes or until tender, stirring occasionally. Yield: 4 servings (serving size: ¾ cup).

quick tip: Look for packages of trimmed, prewashed cauliflower flowerets in your grocer's produce department to keep prep time to a minimum. You can also use about one-half of a head of cauliflower to get 4 cups flowerets.

Skillet Poblano Corn photo, facing page

POINTS:
1

exchanges:
1 Starch
½ Fat

per serving:
Calories 83
Carbohydrate 16.5g
Fat 2.2g (saturated 1.1g)
Fiber 2.2g
Protein 2.5g
Cholesterol 5mg
Sodium 259mg
Calcium 11mg
Iron 0.8mg

Cooking spray
4 teaspoons light stick butter, divided
1 cup seeded, chopped poblano chile peppers, divided (about
    2 peppers)
3 cups frozen whole-kernel corn, thawed and divided
1 teaspoon ground cumin, divided
½ teaspoon salt

1. Coat a large nonstick skillet with cooking spray; add 2 teaspoons light butter, and melt over medium-high heat. Add ½ cup chopped chiles, and cook, stirring constantly, 3 minutes or until tender. Add 1½ cups corn and ½ teaspoon cumin; cook 2 minutes, stirring constantly. Transfer corn mixture to a large serving bowl; cover and keep warm.

2. Repeat procedure with remaining ingredients. Add to reserved corn mixture. Toss with salt. Yield: 5 servings (serving size: ½ cup).

cooking secret: Cooking the corn and pepper in batches allows the vegetables plenty of room in the skillet so that they develop a savory smoked flavor.

**Sweet-and-Sour
Brussels Sprouts with Bacon**
recipe, page 169

Gingered Orange Beets
recipe, page 167

Asparagus Spears with
Garlic Aïoli
recipe, page 165

Braised Peas with Dill

1 tablespoon light stick butter
1 cup finely chopped green onions (about 4 large)
1 (16-ounce) package frozen baby green peas
1 cup fat-free, reduced-sodium chicken broth
⅓ cup chopped fresh dill

1. Melt butter in a medium saucepan over medium heat; add green onions. Cook 1 minute. Add peas and broth; bring to a boil. Cover, reduce heat, and simmer 5 minutes. Stir in dill, and simmer 5 additional minutes or until peas are tender. Serve with a slotted spoon. Yield: 6 servings (serving size: ½ cup).

quick tip: Make sure you select delicate baby green peas for this side dish.

POINTS:
1

exchanges:
1 Starch

per serving:
Calories 75
Carbohydrate 12.3g
Fat 1.0g (saturated 0.7g)
Fiber 3.8g
Protein 4.3g
Cholesterol 3mg
Sodium 232mg
Calcium 28mg
Iron 1.2mg

prep: 20 minutes   cook: 25 minutes

Stuffed Red Peppers

POINTS:

3

exchanges:

1 Starch

1 Vegetable

1 Fat

per serving:

Calories 147

Carbohydrate 20.0g

Fat 5.0g (saturated 2.5g)

Fiber 2.1g

Protein 5.5g

Cholesterol 15mg

Sodium 431mg

Calcium 127mg

Iron 1.1mg

2   large red bell peppers (about 1 pound)

¾   cup finely chopped onion

3   garlic cloves, minced

1   teaspoon light stick butter

1½ cups soft breadcrumbs (about 3¼ slices bread)

½   cup (2 ounces) crumbled tomato-basil feta cheese

⅓   cup fat-free milk

¼   teaspoon salt

1. Cut peppers in half lengthwise. Remove and discard seeds and membranes.

2. Cook pepper cups in boiling water to cover 5 minutes. Drain and set aside.

3. Cook onion and garlic in butter in a skillet over medium heat 5 minutes or until tender, stirring constantly.

4. Combine onion mixture, breadcrumbs, and remaining 3 ingredients in a medium bowl. Spoon ¾ cup onion-breadcrumb mixture into each pepper cup. Place pepper cups in an 11- x 7-inch baking dish. Bake, uncovered, at 400° for 20 minutes. Increase heat to broil. Broil 3 minutes or until lightly browned. Yield: 4 servings (serving size: 1 stuffed pepper cup).

super food: While citrus fruits commonly are associated with vitamin C, bell peppers also are an excellent source of this important nutrient.

New Potatoes in Seasoned Butter

1 pound new potatoes, unpeeled and quartered

1 tablespoon light stick butter

1½ teaspoons lime juice

¾ teaspoon paprika

½ teaspoon salt

3 tablespoons chopped fresh parsley

POINTS:

2

exchanges:

1½ Starch

per serving:

Calories 105

Carbohydrate 21.0g

Fat 1.7g (saturated 1.0g)

Fiber 2.0g

Protein 2.8g

Cholesterol 5mg

Sodium 319mg

Calcium 13mg

Iron 1.1mg

1. Steam potatoes, covered, 6 minutes or until tender. Transfer to a large serving bowl, and keep warm.

2. Combine butter and next 3 ingredients in a small bowl; stir well. Add to potatoes, and toss gently. Sprinkle potatoes with parsley, and toss again. Serve immediately. Yield: 4 servings (serving size: about ⅔ cup).

quick tip: We left the peel on these new potatoes for added flavor and fiber.

prep: 12 minutes   cook: 18 minutes

Dilled Mashed Potatoes

POINTS:

3

exchanges:

1½ Starch

½ Fat

per serving:

Calories 156

Carbohydrate 25.1g

Fat 3.6g (saturated 2.4g)

Fiber 1.7g

Protein 6.6g

Cholesterol 11.6mg

Sodium 458mg

Calcium 139mg

Iron 0.5mg

1½ pounds Yukon Gold potatoes, peeled and sliced into ¼-inch slices

½   cup 1% low-fat milk, warmed

½   cup (2 ounces) shredded reduced-fat sharp Cheddar cheese

1   tablespoon light stick butter, softened

¼   teaspoon dried dill

¾   teaspoon salt

⅛   teaspoon pepper

2   tablespoons finely chopped fresh parsley

1. Place potato in a large saucepan; add water to cover. Bring to a boil; partially cover, reduce heat, and simmer 12 minutes or until tender. Drain potatoes, and return to saucepan.

2. Place saucepan over very low heat; add milk and next 5 ingredients. Mash potatoes with a potato masher; stir in parsley. Yield: 5 servings (serving size: 1 cup).

quick tip: Yukon Golds are a delicious potato variety, prized for their naturally sweet buttery flavor. Like all potatoes, they are high in potassium.

Celeriac Mashed Potatoes

1¼ pounds celeriac, peeled and cut into 1-inch pieces
1¼ pounds russet potatoes, peeled and cut into 1-inch pieces
2   tablespoons light stick butter
¼   cup 2% reduced-fat milk
1   teaspoon salt
¼   teaspoon pepper

1. Place celeriac and potato in a medium saucepan; add water to cover. Bring to a boil; cover, reduce heat, and simmer 20 to 25 minutes or until both are tender. Drain.

2. Pour celeriac and potato into a large bowl, and mash slightly with a potato masher. Add butter and remaining 3 ingredients; mash with potato masher until thoroughly blended. (Mixture will not be completely smooth.) Yield: 6 servings (serving size: ¾ cup).

quick tip: Celeriac, or celery root, is a rather unusual vegetable—knobby, hairy, and brown. Its intriguing texture combines the crunch of celery with the smoothness of potatoes. To prepare, simply trim the ends and peel away the rough exterior.

POINTS:

3

exchanges:
1½ Starch
1 Vegetable
½ Fat

per serving:
Calories 142
Carbohydrate 27.9g
Fat 2.5g (saturated 1.5g)
Fiber 2.7g
Protein 3.6g
Cholesterol 8mg
Sodium 489mg
Calcium 45mg
Iron 0.8mg

Roasted Sweet Potatoes and Onions

POINTS:
2

exchanges:
1½ Starch
½ Fat

per serving:
Calories 121
Carbohydrate 23.2g
Fat 2.6g (saturated 0.4g)
Fiber 2.2g
Protein 1.8g
Cholesterol 0mg
Sodium 158mg
Calcium 26mg
Iron 0.6mg

1 large sweet potato, peeled and cut into ½-inch cubes
1 medium onion, cut into ½-inch wedges
2 teaspoons extra-virgin olive oil
¼ teaspoon salt
⅛ teaspoon pepper
Cooking spray

1. Combine first 5 ingredients in a large bowl; toss well.

2. Coat a nonstick baking sheet with cooking spray; add potato mixture, and arrange in a single layer.

3. Bake at 400° for 20 to 25 minutes or until potato is tender, stirring once. Serve immediately. Yield: 4 servings (serving size: ½ cup).

super food: Sweet potatoes are one of nature's most nutrient-dense foods. Loaded with fiber, vitamin C, and especially beta-carotene, sweet potatoes are among the top good-for-you foods.

Cumin-Scented Squash

2   fresh yellow squash, halved lengthwise
1   tablespoon olive oil
¼   teaspoon ground cumin
¼   teaspoon salt
⅛   teaspoon ground red pepper

POINTS:

1

exchanges:

1 Vegetable
½ Fat

1. Place squash halves, cut side up, on a baking sheet; drizzle with oil. Bake at 450° for 20 minutes.

2. Cook cumin in a small skillet over medium heat, stirring and shaking often, 3 to 4 minutes or until fragrant. Combine cumin, salt, and red pepper in a small bowl. Sprinkle over squash. Yield: 4 servings (serving size: 1 squash half).

cooking secret: Pungent, sharp, and slightly bitter, cumin is a common ingredient in Indian spice blends and Mexican foods. Like other spices, it should be stored in a cool place and away from heat.

per serving:

Calories 48
Carbohydrate 3.9g
Fat 3.6g (saturated 0.5g)
Fiber 1.7g
Protein 1.1g
Cholesterol 0mg
Sodium 149mg
Calcium 19mg
Iron 0.5mg

Stewed Butternut Squash

POINTS:

1

exchanges:

1 Starch

per serving:

Calories 83
Carbohydrate 17.8g
Fat 1.7g (saturated 1.0g)
Fiber 4.1g
Protein 1.7g
Cholesterol 5mg
Sodium 220mg
Calcium 61mg
Iron 0.9mg

1½ tablespoons light stick butter
1¼ cups chopped sweet onion (about 1 medium)
1 (1½-pound) butternut squash, peeled, seeded, and cut into
   1½-inch pieces
2 tablespoons dark brown sugar
½ teaspoon salt
1 teaspoon chopped fresh thyme
½ cup water

1. Melt butter in a medium saucepan over medium heat. Add onion, and cook 5 minutes or until tender and golden. Add squash and remaining 4 ingredients.

2. Bring to a boil; cover, reduce heat, and simmer 20 minutes or until squash is tender. Yield: 6 servings (serving size: ⅔ cup).

cooking secret: Microwave the whole butternut squash about 1 minute on HIGH so that it's softer and easier to cut.

Baked Dijon Tomatoes

Cooking spray

2 medium tomatoes, halved crosswise (about 8 ounces each)

2 teaspoons light mayonnaise

2 teaspoons Dijon mustard

Dash of ground red pepper

¼ cup Italian breadcrumbs

2 tablespoons chopped fresh parsley

2 tablespoons freshly grated Parmesan cheese

POINTS:

2

exchanges:

½ Starch

1 Vegetable

½ Fat

per serving:

Calories 84

Carbohydrate 12.3g

Fat 2.9g (saturated 0.8g)

Fiber 1.9g

Protein 3.7g

Cholesterol 3mg

Sodium 263mg

Calcium 66mg

Iron 1.2mg

1. Coat a nonstick baking sheet with cooking spray. Place tomatoes, cut side up, on baking sheet.

2. Combine mayonnaise, mustard, and red pepper in a small bowl; stir well. Set aside.

3. Combine breadcrumbs, parsley, and cheese.

4. Spread about 1 teaspoon mayonnaise mixture on cut sides of each tomato. Top each tomato evenly with breadcrumb mixture. Bake at 400° for 12 to 15 minutes or just until tomato is tender. Remove from oven, and let stand 5 minutes before serving. Yield: 4 servings (serving size: 1 tomato half).

super food: Tomatoes are one of the best foods you can eat, thanks to their vitamin C and lycopene content. So, make tomatoes a staple in your diet, from salsa to sauce to this simple side.

Caramelized Turnips

POINTS:

1

exchanges:

1½ Vegetable

per serving:

Calories 39

Carbohydrate 7.3g

Fat 1.1g (saturated 0.7g)

Fiber 1.7g

Protein 0.8g

Cholesterol 3mg

Sodium 251mg

Calcium 23mg

Iron 0.3mg

1   tablespoon light stick butter

1¾ pounds turnips, peeled and coarsely chopped (about 3 turnips)

1½ tablespoons sugar

1   cup water

½   teaspoon salt

¼   cup minced fresh parsley

1. Melt butter in a large nonstick skillet over medium-high heat; add turnips. Cook 10 minutes or until turnips are browned.

2. Add sugar; cook 30 seconds, stirring constantly. Add water and salt; stir well. Simmer, uncovered, 10 minutes or until most of the liquid is absorbed and turnips are tender. Transfer turnips to a large serving bowl; sprinkle with parsley, and toss gently. Yield: 6 servings (serving size: ⅔ cup).

quick tip: Turnips are round with whitish skin and a purple band. Fresh turnips are available year-round. Look for roots that are smooth, firm, and heavy for their size. Store roots in a cool, moist area or in a plastic bag in the crisper drawer of your refrigerator.

Mexican Zucchini and Corn

1   tablespoon olive oil
2   cups halved and thinly sliced onion (about 1 medium)
2   garlic cloves, minced
5   cups halved and thinly sliced zucchini (about 3 medium)
1   (15¼-ounce) can whole-kernel corn, rinsed and drained
1   chipotle pepper in adobo sauce, drained, seeded, and chopped
½   teaspoon dried oregano
½   teaspoon salt

POINTS:
1

exchanges:
½ Starch
1 Vegetable
½ Fat

per serving:
Calories 85
Carbohydrate 14.5g
Fat 2.9g (saturated 0.4g)
Fiber 2.7g
Protein 2.8g
Cholesterol 0mg
Sodium 294mg
Calcium 28mg
Iron 1.0mg

1. Heat oil in a large nonstick skillet over medium-high heat until hot. Add onion and garlic; cook, stirring constantly, 2 to 3 minutes or until tender.

2. Add zucchini. Cook 6 to 7 minutes or until zucchini is lightly browned and tender.

3. Stir in corn and remaining 3 ingredients. Cook 6 to 8 minutes, stirring occasionally. Yield: 6 servings (serving size: 1 cup).

cooking secret: If you prefer mildly spicy dishes, simply use one-half chipotle pepper, seeded and chopped.

Roasted Vegetables

POINTS:
1

exchanges:
1½ Vegetable
½ Fat

per serving:
Calories 60
Carbohydrate 8.8g
Fat 2.7g (saturated 0.4g)
Fiber 2.2g
Protein 1.6g
Cholesterol 0mg
Sodium 247mg
Calcium 18mg
Iron 0.7mg

Olive oil-flavored cooking spray
1   red bell pepper, cut into 1-inch pieces
1   yellow bell pepper, cut into 1-inch pieces
1   small yellow onion, cut into ½-inch wedges and separated
1   medium zucchini, cut into ½-inch-thick slices
2   medium tomatoes, seeded and cut into 1-inch cubes
1   chipotle pepper in adobo sauce, drained, seeded, and finely chopped
1   tablespoon extra-virgin olive oil
¼   teaspoon salt
¼   teaspoon freshly ground pepper

1. Cover baking sheet with heavy-duty aluminum foil; coat with cooking spray. Arrange bell peppers, onion, zucchini, and tomato on baking sheet; coat vegetables with cooking spray. Broil 3 inches from heat 16 minutes, stirring once. Remove vegetables from baking sheet, and transfer to a large serving bowl.

2. Combine chipotle pepper and remaining 3 ingredients in a small bowl; stir with a whisk until blended. Pour over warm vegetables; toss gently to coat. Serve warm or chilled. Yield: 6 servings (serving size: ½ cup).

 quick tip: Roasting is one of the simplest cooking methods and one of the best ways to preserve the vitamin content in vegetables. It also brings out a food's natural sweetness.

Recipe Index

Acknowledgments & Credits

A'Mano,
Mountain Brook, AL

At Home Furnishings,
Homewood, AL

Table Matters,
Mountain Brook, AL

Sources of Nutrient Analysis Data:

Computrition, Inc.,
Chatsworth, CA

The Food Processor by ESHA Research,
Salem, OR

Information provided by food manufacturers

Metric Equivalents

The recipes that appear in this cookbook use the standard United States method for measuring liquid and dry or solid ingredients (teaspoons, tablespoons, and cups). The information in the following charts is provided to help cooks outside the U.S. successfully use these recipes. All equivalents are approximate.

Equivalents for Different Types of Ingredients

A standard cup measure of a dry or solid ingredient will vary in weight depending on the type of ingredient. A standard cup of liquid is the same volume for any type of liquid. Use the following chart when converting standard cup measures to grams (weight) or milliliters (volume).

Standard Cup	Fine Powder (ex. flour)	Grain (ex. rice)	Granular (ex. sugar)	Liquid Solids (ex. butter)	Liquid (ex. milk)
1	140 g	150 g	190 g	200 g	240 ml
¾	105 g	113 g	143 g	150 g	180 ml
⅔	93 g	100 g	125 g	133 g	160 ml
½	70 g	75 g	95 g	100 g	120 ml
⅓	47 g	50 g	63 g	67 g	80 ml
¼	35 g	38 g	48 g	50 g	60 ml
⅛	18 g	19 g	24 g	25 g	30 ml

Dry Ingredients by Weight

(To convert ounces to grams, multiply the number of ounces by 30.)

1 oz	=	¹⁄₁₆ lb	=	30 g
4 oz	=	¼ lb	=	120 g
8 oz	=	½ lb	=	240 g
12 oz	=	¾ lb	=	360 g
16 oz	=	1 lb	=	480 g

Length

(To convert inches to centimeters, multiply the number of inches by 2.5.)

1 in =				= 2.5 cm			
6 in =	½ ft			= 15 cm			
12 in =	1 ft			= 30 cm			
36 in =	3 ft	= 1 yd	=	90 cm			
40 in =				= 100 cm	= 1 meter		

Liquid Ingredients by Volume

¼ tsp	=					1 ml
½ tsp	=					2 ml
1 tsp	=					5 ml
3 tsp	= 1 tbls		= ½ fl oz	=	15 ml
	2 tbls	= ⅛ cup	= 1 fl oz	=	30 ml
	4 tbls	= ¼ cup	= 2 fl oz	=	60 ml
	5⅓ tbls	= ⅓ cup	= 3 fl oz	=	80 ml
	8 tbls	= ½ cup	= 4 fl oz	=	120 ml
	10⅔ tbls	= ⅔ cup	= 5 fl oz	=	160 ml
	12 tbls	= ¾ cup	= 6 fl oz	=	180 ml
	16 tbls	= 1 cup	= 8 fl oz	=	240 ml
1 pt	=	2 cups	= 16 fl oz	=	480 ml
1 qt	=	4 cups	= 32 fl oz	=	960 ml
			33 fl oz	=	1000 ml = 1 liter

Cooking/Oven Temperatures

	Fahrenheit	Celsius	Gas Mark
Freeze Water	32° F	0° C	
Room Temperature	68° F	20° C	
Boil Water	212° F	100° C	
Bake	325° F	160° C	3
	350° F	180° C	4
	375° F	190° C	5
	400° F	200° C	6
	425° F	220° C	7
	450° F	230° C	8
Broil			Grill